S0-DVC-207

BEST OF THE BEST

BASEBALL

35 Major League Superstars

Text by Ken Rosenthal

Produced in partnership with and licensed by
MAJOR LEAGUE BASEBALL PROPERTIES, INC.

Published by Masters Press
A Division of Howard W. Sams and Company

This edition published 1998 by Masters Press
A Division of Howard W. Sams and Company
2647 Waterfront Parkway East Drive, Indianapolis, Indiana 46214 U.S.A.
Copyright © 1998 by Lionheart Books, LTD.
Produced in partnership with and licensed by
MAJOR LEAGUE BASEBALL PROPERTIES, INC.

MLB Credits
Editor, Publishing—*Gary Perkinson*
Assistant Editor, Publishing—*Mike McCormick*
Manager, Major League Baseball Photos—*Rich Pilling*
Project Photo Editor/Administrator, Major League Baseball Photos—*Paul Cunningham*

Produced by Lionheart Books, Ltd., Atlanta, Georgia 30341
Design—*Carley Wilson Brown*

Cover photo—*Ron Vesely*

All rights reserved. No part of this book may be reproduced, stored in a retrieval system,
or transmitted in any form or by any means, electronic, mechanical, photocopying, recording,
or otherwise, without the prior permission of Masters Press.
Printed in the United States of America
International Standard Book Number: 1-57028-207-2

10   9   8   7   6   5   4   3   2   1

Contents

Roberto Alomar

SECOND BASE—BALTIMORE ORIOLES

R oberto Alomar does things on a baseball field you've never seen before. Things you don't necessarily notice. Things you don't even imagine.

The Baltimore Orioles second baseman will dive to both his left and right to stab ground balls, turning hits into outs.

He will throw behind a runner at third, trying to catch him as he rounds the bag toward home.

And he also will make split-second judgments at the plate, stealing a glance at the third baseman while a pitcher is in his windup before deciding to bunt.

"He doesn't go against the book," former Major League pitcher Mike Flanagan once said. "He's adding chapters to the book."

Like Cal Ripken Jr., Alomar displays the special instincts of a player who grew up in a baseball family. And like Ken Griffey Jr., he's blessed with even more physical talent than his father.

Sandy Alomar Sr. played 15 years in the Majors, but he'll probably be remembered most for raising two All-Star sons.

Sandy Jr., a catcher for the Cleveland Indians, would go through stages where he preferred dirt bikes and volleyball growing up in Puerto Rico. Robbie, the younger brother, always wanted to play baseball. Robbie was the natural.

When a St. Louis Cardinals scout saw him playing pepper at the age of 6, he asked Sandy Sr., "Can I sign him now?" More than two decades later, little has changed.

[
*"He doesn't go against
the book. He's adding chapters
to the book."*
]

I play to win. God has given me a gift to play this game, and I work at it." — *Roberto Alomar, Baltimore Orioles*

"It's almost eerie how good he is," said John Stearns, one of Alomar's coaches in his first two seasons with the Orioles.

There is an acrobatic, ballet-like quality to Alomar's game, especially when he's in the field. But what distinguishes him is his knack for rising to the occasion, his flair for the dramatic.

Few players can dominate a game physically as well as intellectually. Alomar, a switch-hitter with speed, is dangerous on many levels—and never more dangerous than when the stakes are highest.

"He has that special ability that every young player and old player like myself wishes they had, and they're ashamed that they only wish that they could

be like that," said catcher Mark Parent, one of Alomar's former teammates.

Alomar, 30, first demonstrated that ability on a grand scale in the 1992 American League playoffs. His game-tying home run off Oakland's Dennis Eckersley in Game 4 was a turning point in Toronto Blue Jays history.

The Blue Jays went on to win back-to-back World Series, and Alomar returned to the Post Season with the Orioles in 1996, under remarkably different circumstances.

Fans in two countries turned on Alomar after he spit on umpire John Hirschbeck in Toronto. He was booed and criticized even after he apologized for his mistake. Yet, his play during that tumultous period barely suffered.

The day after the spitting incident, Alomar hit a 10th-inning homer to clinch the Orioles' first Post Season berth in 13 years.

He then went one better in the decisive game of the Division Series against Cleveland, delivering a game-tying single in the ninth and a game-winning homer in the 12th.

Afterward, Sandy Jr. embraced his brother and opponent. Roberto burst into tears.

The great ones maintain an unusual level of calm when the pressure is highest, but Alomar was a man on an island, and he still rescued his team.

He looked forward to a fresh start in 1997, but injuries limited him. Alomar could not bat right-handed after May 31 due to a shoulder problem. Still, he hit a pivotal two-run double against a left-hander in the playoffs—batting left-handed.

That's Alomar, never lacking nerve, always full of surprises.

His game is both subtle and spectacular. Watch him throw—his arm is so strong, even his patented back-handed "shovel" flips to second zoom across the field. Watch him steal bases—he reads pitchers

so effectively, he gets some of the biggest jumps you'll ever see. "He takes off before pitchers even let go of the ball," Orioles catcher Chris Hoiles said.

Years from now, fans will recall one marvelous play or another and say, "I saw Roberto Alomar do that." He's that creative, that unusual, that special.

Roberto Alomar/2B — Baltimore Orioles

	1997	CAREER
POS	2B	2B
B	S	S
G	112	1416
AVG	.333	.304
AB	412	5460
H	137	1659
2B	23	339
3B	2	54
HR	14	113
RBI	60	653
R	64	893
SB	9	322
BB	40	600
SO	43	630

Sandy Alomar

CATCHER—CLEVELAND INDIANS

He earned his amazing 1997 season from his 30-game hitting streak to his All-Star Most Valuable Player award from his career-high offensive statistics to his dramatic hits in the Post Season.

"It's an all Sandy Alomar season," Cleveland Indians shortstop Omar Vizquel said during the World Series. "The Spanish word is *magico*. Magic."

Alomar Jr. suffered through the Indians' lean years, endured five straight injury-marred seasons, and wondered if he would ever fulfill the promise of his 1990 Rookie of the Year award.

Now, after catching back-to-back 100-game seasons for the first time as a Major leaguer, he knows the answer.

"I'm glad that I'm healthy now," he said. "I can show the whole world that I can play baseball."

Most everyone knew that before—Alomar, 31, is a five-time All-Star and former Gold Glove winner—but injuries threatened to ruin his career.

He was the only player in the Majors to spend time on the disabled list every season from 1991 to 1995. During that period, he averaged only 70 games per year.

He underwent four knee surgeries and one back surgery. He damaged his rotator-cuff. He strained a hip flexor. He twice tore the webbing between his right ring and middle fingers.

Part of the problem was his size—at 6-foot-5 and 215 pounds, Alomar is the game's tallest starting catcher. Bigger catchers get hit with more foul balls.

"The Spanish word is magico.
Magic."

I'm glad that I'm healthy now. I can show the whole world that I can play baseball."
—*Sandy Alomar, Cleveland Indians*

"*The success he's having couldn't happen to a better guy...*"

"I put my entire trust in him," said Charles Nagy, who has worked with Alomar for seven seasons, the longest of any Indians pitcher. "He knows me better than I know myself."

Still, Alomar's defense was the least discussed part of his game last season. He batted .324 with 37 doubles, 21 home runs and 83 RBIs—a stunning breakout for a player who began the year with a .270 career average and only 53 homers.

The new Alomar hit home runs in five consecutive

They also stand a greater risk of injury in collisions at home plate.

"It was real frustrating for Sandy," said his younger brother, Roberto, the Baltimore Orioles second baseman. "I know he can do much better than he's done. But he has played through the pain."

How much skill did Sandy lose?

"I wish I knew. I really wish I knew. I know I could have been much better behind the plate. I know I could do a lot of things like Pudge Rodriguez does— snap throws to first and pickoff attempts."

So, rather than return to his native Puerto Rico for winter ball, Alomar spent the '96-'97 off-season in Cleveland, working with Indians strength coach Fernando Montes, preparing himself "like a boxer in a major fight."

The results showed in every aspect of his play. As Alomar regained confidence, the Cleveland pitchers regained their confidence in him. And in October, his pitch selection helped an average staff reach the seventh game of the World Series.

games. Ended a perfect game by Orioles ace Mike Mussina in the ninth inning. Produced the second-longest hitting streak by a catcher in Major League history.

Then came the Post Season.

Alomar hit a game-tying home run off the New York Yankees' Mariano Rivera with the Indians four outs away from elimination in the Division Series.

He hit a two-out, game-winning single off the Orioles' Armando Benitez in the ninth inning of Game 4 of the American League Championship Series.

And then he batted .367 against the Florida Marlins in the World Series, finishing the Post Season with a team-high five homers and 19 RBIs in 18 games.

"The success he's having couldn't happen to a better guy," Indians general manager John Hart said. "All those years of injuries. To watch and witness

what he did in the off-season, coming into the weight room at 10 a.m. every day, it makes this even more special."

Magical.

Sandy Alomar/C — Cleveland Indians

	1997	CAREER
POS	C	C
B	R	R
G	125	742
AVG	.324	.280
AB	451	2527
H	146	707
2B	37	140
3B	0	4
HR	21	74
RBI	83	348
R	63	309
SB	0	22
BB	19	130
SO	48	281

It's a game. But sometimes until you get hurt and sit back and watch, you forget that."
—*Jeff Bagwell, Houston Astros*

Jeff Bagwell

FIRST BASE—HOUSTON ASTROS

It was bad enough when the Boston Red Sox sold Babe Ruth. But 71 years later, they perpetuated the "Curse of the Bambino," trading Jeff Bagwell.

At the time, Bagwell was a Double-A third baseman stuck behind Wade Boggs, Scott Cooper and Tim Naehring in the Boston farm system.

Who knew the New England native would become a Rookie of the Year, Most Valuable Player and three-time All-Star? Certainly not the Red Sox.

Larry Andersen was the left-handed reliever they needed to hold off Toronto in the 1990 American League East pennant race, and they made the deal.

Andersen did his part, posting a 1.23 ERA in 15 games. But he left the team as a free agent after Boston lost in the playoffs. And Bagwell, after moving to first base, turned downright Ruthian.

He grew up in Middletown, Connecticut, attended the University of Hartford and dreamed of playing for the Red Sox. But when the trade was made, the 6-foot, 195-pound Bagwell had hit only six home runs in 711 Minor League at-bats.

His acquistion wasn't even Major news in Houston—the Astros sent longtime second baseman Bill Doran to Cincinnati the same day, reducing the Anderson-for-Bagwell deal to a footnote.

"Sitting in the general manager's chair when you make a trade like that, you hope to get someone who can make a contribution at the Major League level—period," former Houston GM Bill Wood said.

Well, in seven seasons with the Astros, Bagwell

Who knew the New England native would become a Rookie of the Year, Most Valuable Player and three-time All-Star?

"*A lot of times, a lot of us in baseball take for granted what we do for a living.*"

has contributed 187 home runs, 246 doubles, 724 RBIs and a .304 batting average—not bad, considering he suffered a broken left hand three straight years.

Each of the injuries occurred the same way, when the right-handed hitting Bagwell was struck by a fastball while looking for a slider. Ben Rivera hit him in '93, Andy Benes in '94, Brian Williams in '95.

"I'd never been hurt before that," Bagwell said. "The first time was, 'I can't believe that happened.' The second time, it was like, 'Not again. You've got to be kidding me.' The third time was like, 'No, this is bad.'"

Bagwell, 30, decided a change was necessary, but he didn't move off the plate or pull back his hands on inside pitches. He just started wearing a new batting glove featuring an air-cushioned pad.

The past two seasons showed what he can accomplish when he plays 162 games. In 1996, he set team records in extra-base hits, total bases and RBIs. And in '97, he did it again.

"No one gets locked in for longer periods. We just jump on and ride the train," said Bagwell's teammate

and fellow 'Killer B,' Astros second baseman Craig Biggio.

Biggio predicted that Bagwell could hit 50 to 60 home runs every season if he played in a more favorable hitter's park than the Astrodome. Bagwell doesn't engage in such projections. He's just happy to be healthy again.

"A lot of times, a lot of us in baseball take for granted what we do for a living," Bagwell said. "We don't think about how much fun this can be, doing what we did as kids and what we always wanted to do. It's a game. But sometimes until you get hurt and sit

back and watch, you forget that."

A similar lesson applied after the Houston trade, which Bagwell initially viewed as "devastating." He grew up such a Red Sox fan, he would pretend to be Carl Yastrzemski. And he was named MVP of the Eastern League after batting .333 for Double-A New Britain.

"That was tough," Bagwell said, recalling the day of the trade. "My mother's crying. My grandmother's crying. I'm living at home and playing Double A. After that, it's Pawtucket (R.I.) and then Boston. I'm two hours from my home."

Bagwell's father was the voice of reason, reminding his son that the Astros would give him a chance to play. And at his MVP news conference in 1994, Bagwell said, "It turned out to be the best thing that could have happened to me."

He became only the third unanimous National League MVP in that strike-shortened season, and still doesn't appear to have reached his peak.

It was bad enough that the Red Sox sold Babe Ruth. But did they have to trade Jeff Bagwell?

Jeff Bagwell/1B — Houston Astros

	1997	CAREER
POS	1B	1B
B	R	R
G	162	1008
AVG	.286	.304
AB	566	3657
H	162	1112
2B	40	246
3B	2	20
HR	43	187
RBI	135	724
R	109	654
SB	31	109
BB	127	627
SO	122	689

When I look at a pitcher, I can tell if he's feeling confident or a little shaky."—*Albert Belle, Chicago White Sox*

Albert Belle

OUTFIELD—CHICAGO WHITE SOX

Albert Belle isn't simply one of the most dangerous hitters in baseball. He's one of the most studious, too.

Belle charts every pitch thrown to him, using index cards to keep notes on opposing pitchers. He also watches videotape to help correct flaws in his swing.

John Hart, Belle's former general manager in Cleveland, once called him, "the most focused player I've been around." Carlos Baerga, a former Indians teammate, said, "Nobody works harder on hitting, except maybe Tony Gwynn."

Belle's controversial image sometimes overshadows his baseball talent, but there's no denying his ability to affect the outcome of a game.

In the strike-shortened 1995 season, he became the only player in Major-league history to hit 50 homers and 50 doubles in the same season. In '96, he led the majors with 148 RBIs, matching the sixth highest total since 1949.

Last season was Belle's first with the Chicago White Sox. He batted .274 with 30 homers and 116 RBIs. His 76 extra-base hits were one shy of the team record. Yet, he described it at as "a bad season . . . a roller-coaster year."

"Physically and mentally, I'm exhausted by the end of every game. I go home and look in the mirror and say, 'What else could I have done today?'"

Belle, 31, was born in Shreveport, Louisiana. Both of his parents are educators. He studied French

[
*"He's the most focused player
I have ever been around."*
]

among other subjects in high school, and graduated sixth in a class of 266.

Of course, his intelligence wouldn't help him as a hitter if he didn't also possess the physical tools — superb vision, tremendously quick hands, exceptional bat speed.

The 6-foot-2, 210-pound Belle is three inches shorter and 50 pounds lighter than his fellow White Sox slugger, Frank Thomas. But he's even more fearsome, in his own way.

The sight of Belle at the plate is unmistakable. He glares toward the mound, waving his bat like a club. When the pitch comes, he explodes out of his crouch, extends his powerful arms and makes contact.

The sight of Belle at the plate is unmistakable.

"He plays the game with controlled aggression," San Diego Padres coach Davey Lopes once said. "That's what I like about Albert Belle. He wants to beat your butt. You can see it."

It all starts with his stare. Belle sizes up a pitcher the way a heavyweight boxer sizes up an opponent, seeking to intimidate before a pitch is even thrown.

"I was never really conscious I did that until somebody brought it up to me in college," referring to his days at LSU. "But when I look at a pitcher, I can tell if he's feeling confident or a little shaky."

And then the at-bat begins.

The problem with pitching to Belle is that he can hit any pitch out of the park at any time. Throw him a neck-high, 93-mph fastball that is several inches outside, and he still might hit an opposite-field home run.

"When Albert first came up, he had a hitch in his swing," the Baltimore Orioles' Joe Carter said. "It looked like he could hit a curveball, but I wondered if he'd be able to handle a Major League fastball. Boy, was I wrong."

Belle is the only player in baseball to hit at least 30 home runs in each of the last six seasons. He reached 200 home runs in 2,893 at-bats, the sixth-fastest pace in Major League history.

Yet, he isn't merely a slugger. Belle had a 27-game hitting streak last season, tying a White Sox record.

And he batted .357 in the strike-shortened '94 season, finishing two points behind Paul O'Neill for the American League batting title.

He studies pitchers. He watches tapes. He locks in.

"Albert Belle has a tremendously powerful mind and ability to focus in, to keep in what he wants in and shut out what he doesn't," former White Sox manager Terry Bevington said.

It's called concentration. And for all of Belle's physical attributes, it might be his biggest weapon.

Albert Belle/OF — Chicago White Sox

	1997	CAREER
POS	OF	OF
B	R	R
G	161	1074
AVG	.274	.292
AB	634	4075
H	174	1188
2B	45	268
3B	1	17
HR	30	272
RBI	116	867
R	90	682
SB	4	65
BB	53	449
SO	105	727

I want the team to succeed here. We're going to make it work and win a championship."
— *Craig Biggio, Houston Astros*

Craig Biggio

SECOND BASE—HOUSTON ASTROS

The defining moment of Craig Biggio's career wasn't a game-winning homer or a game-saving stop at second base.

For Biggio, a never-say-die, win-at-all-costs competitor, it occurred when he beat out a double play.

The National League trailed the 1994 All-Star Game, 7-5, when the Houston second baseman came to bat with one on and none out in the ninth inning.

Facing Lee Smith, Biggio fouled off three pitches with two strikes. He then hit a sharp grounder to Scott Cooper at third.

Cooper misplayed the ball slightly, but got the force at second. Biggio, running hard as always, beat the throw to first.

The next batter, Fred McGriff, tied the score with a two-run homer, and the National League went on to win in 10 innings, 8-7.

"That was the big play, Biggio beating out the double play," said McGriff, who was named the game's MVP.

A big play that resulted from a sheer act of hustle, one of those "little things" that often affect the outcomes of games.

Biggio, 32, is the only player in Major League history to make the All-Star team at catcher and second base. He has produced three 20-homer seasons and four 30-stolen base seasons. And in 1997, he scored 146 runs, the most by a National League player in 65 years.

Even with all that, what distinguishes the Long Island native is his true-grit style. Biggio runs out

[
If there's anyone who was born to play baseball, it's Craig Biggio.
]

21

> *What distinguishes the
> Long Island native is his
> true-grit style.*

straight Gold Gloves. Looking back, he called the decision to change positions "a cakewalk" compared to the one he faced as a free agent at the end of the '95 season.

Colorado, St. Louis and San Diego all wanted Biggio, but he accepted less money to stay in Houston, the team that selected him in the first round of the 1987 draft out of Seton Hall.

His announcement was a Major relief to the city at a time when the NFL Oilers were negotiating to move to Nashville and the Astros' future also was in jeopardy.

"I think there would have been a good chance the team wouldn't have been in Houston much longer if

every ball. He has even led the NL in hit-by-pitches the last three years.

"If there's anyone who was born to play baseball," Astros manager Larry Dierker said, "it's Craig Biggio."

And if Biggio didn't possess that inner drive, he never could have converted to second base after spending his first five professional seasons at catcher.

The Astros asked him to make the switch, believing a 5-foot-11, 180-pound player could better realize his offensive potential at a less physically demanding position.

"It scared the daylights out of me," Biggio said. "If I had fallen on my face, then what would have happened? What fueled my fire was that nobody thought I could do it. That was my whole inspiration."

Two years later, Biggio won his first of four

Craig had left," former Astros pitcher Greg Swindell said. "I don't know what we would have done without him."

Houstonians probably couldn't have imagined it, either.

Biggio won the 1997 Branch Rickey Award for community service. He is involved with nearly a dozen charities, most notably the Sunshine Kids, an organization that provides recreational opportunities and support to children with cancer.

How committed is Biggio? Every year, he joins the children on a ski trip to Denver. Every year, he throws a party for them in the Astrodome.

"I've been a part of this organization for eight years," Biggio said the day he re-signed with the Astros. "When you spend that much time in a city, you become close to a lot of people.

"I want to finish what we started. I want the team to succeed here. We're going to make it work and win a championship. I want to help the city get back on its feet."

It could happen—the Oilers left, but the Astros stayed. Last season, they won their first division title since 1986. And in two years, they'll open a new downtown ballpark.

Fitting, isn't it? Biggio helped his city beat out a double play.

Craig Biggio/2B — Houston Astros

	1997	CAREER
POS	2B	2B/C/OF
B	R	R
G	162	1379
AVG	.309	.288
AB	619	5104
H	191	1470
2B	37	282
3B	8	36
HR	22	116
RBI	81	545
R	146	874
SB	47	268
BB	84	634
SO	107	753

I'll do what I can do so other players will get the best potential out of themselves."
— *Barry Bonds, San Francisco Giants*

Barry Bonds

OUTFIELD—SAN FRANCISCO GIANTS

Bobby Bonds is his father, Willie Mays his godfather. It was quite a pair to follow, but the first measure of Barry Bonds' greatness is that he actually caught up.

Bonds, 33, still bristles when someone mistakenly calls him "Bobby." But he has surpassed his father's achievements, and now draws comparisons to his godfather, the greatest San Francisco Giant of all.

Mays is perhaps the finest all-around player in Major-League history, Bonds perhaps the finest in the game today. Still, it wasn't always easy being Barry Bonds. Only now is he growing comfortable with his identity.

"I always dreamed of being someone like Michael Jordan and having someone ask me how I felt after a game," Bonds said. "No one ever asked me that kind of question.

"My questions were always from someone wanting to know if I was going to the Major Leagues like my dad. If I thought I was going to be as good as my father was.

"Other athletes got to be themselves their whole lives. I never got to be loved for me."

Yet there was Bonds last September, kneeling in prayer when the Giants clinched the 1997 National League West title, then dancing on the dugout and diving into the arms of fans.

Bonds, one of the game's most complex superstars, is frequently criticized for his moodiness. But his outlook seemed to improve dramatically last

He is a seven-time All-Star and a seven-time Gold Glove winner in left field.

25

> He plays hard,
> and he plays every day.

season, even as he struggled to produce his usual monster numbers.

"The worst season of my career," Bonds called it at one point. Not exactly—Bonds narrowly missed producing an unprecedented second-straight season of 40 homers and 40 steals. Equally significant, another side of him emerged.

"I want to be there in October," he said. "Individual numbers mean nothing to me now. It's better for me to hit behind some guys. Whether it's hitting third, fourth, fifth or sixth, I'll do what I can do so other players will get the best potential out of themselves.

"If I can bat behind a .280 hitter and make him a .300 hitter, that's fine. It's more important to me than 40 home runs and 40 stolen bases. I don't expect to do that again. I've done all that before and the team always came up short."

But this time, the Giants didn't come up short, winning their division by 2½ games. Bonds led the NL in walks for the fourth straight season. Jeff Kent and J.T. Snow, the players batting behind him, enjoyed career years.

At the All-Star Game, Bonds said it was "kind of nice to ride someone else's shoulders for a change." But who was it that carried the Giants in a nine-game stretch that clinched the division, hitting seven homers, driving in 13 runs and scoring 12 more? Bonds.

He yearns to play in the World Series after appearing in three NL Championship Series with Pittsburgh and the 1997 Divison Series with San Francisco. But Bonds wouldn't be Bonds if he wasn't also driven by individual goals.

He is a seven-time All-Star and a seven-time Gold Glove winner in left field. He is also the only player to win three Most Valuable Player awards in four seasons, and the only one to hit 350 homers and steal 350 bases.

Mays, Bobby Bonds and Andre Dawson are the only other 300-300 men in Major League history. Barry seeks to make his own club even more exclusive. He's 26 homers short of 400-400, and musing about the possibility of 500-500.

Ken Griffey Jr. could probably steal 40 bases in a season, but the Seattle Mariners don't ask him to try. Bonds more closely represents the ideal blend of speed and power that scouts seek in a position player.

"Sometimes you shake your head and wonder how he does what he does," San Diego outfielder Tony Gwynn said. "But at the same time, I know he does his homework."

Bonds employs the same personal trainer as the San Francisco 49ers' Jerry Rice. He plays hard and

*Sometimes you shake your head and wonder how he does what he does. . .
but at the same time, I know he does his homework.*

[
"At the end of my career,
I want to make a difference
in the community...."
]

he plays every day, appearing in all but 13 games over the past five seasons.

Off the field, Bonds is nearly as active. He is an elected board member for the United Way of San Francisco. And he is heavily involved with the Adopt a Special Kid organization, which places special-needs children in caring homes.

"At the end of my career, I want to make a difference in the community, especially the black community," Bonds said. "I don't want people to live with

a hardened heart because someone is stomping on it all the time."

Still, Bonds isn't close to retiring, not yet. He has so much more to accomplish. The 500-500 milestone. An unprecedented fourth MVP award. A World Series title.

Earlier in his career, he struggled to forge his own identity, saying he "couldn't handle" the comparisons with his father, Bobby, and godfather, Willie. Now, he's forging his own Hall of Fame legacy.

"To make the Hall of Fame as a player, that's the greatest honor anybody can give you in this game," Bonds said. "I don't feel as if I'm even worthy to go until I'm there.

"As a visitor, you can go visit. But as a player? No way, man. If my dad happened to get in there, I might sit outside the building. But I won't go in there."

His invitation will come soon enough. He's more than just Bobby's son or Willie's godson. He's their worthy heir. He's a star among stars. He's Barry Bonds.

Barry Bonds/OF — San Francisco Giants

	1997	CAREER
POS	OF	OF
B	L	L
G	159	1742
AVG	.291	.288
AB	532	6079
H	155	1750
2B	26	359
3B	5	56
HR	40	374
RBI	101	1094
R	123	1244
SB	37	417
BB	145	1227
SO	87	958

Ken Caminiti

THIRD BASE—SAN DIEGO PADRES

Rarely has a player been so ill before a game. Never has a candy bar been credited with so much healing power.

San Diego's Ken Caminiti won the 1996 National League Most Valuable Player award despite playing nearly the entire season with a torn rotator cuff.

But that wasn't his most impressive physical feat.

Caminiti, 34, cemented his reputation as one of baseball's all-time tough guys on a hot August day in Monterrey, Mexico, when he overcame food poisoning to hit home runs in his first two at-bats.

It was the first time that Major-League teams had played regular-season games in Mexico. And minutes before the series finale, Caminiti laid on the floor of manager Bruce Bochy's office, dehydrated and cramping.

Padres general manager Kevin Towers said he was "white as a ghost." Undaunted, the switch-hitting third baseman took two liters of intravenous fluids, and told Bochy he could play.

After the top of the first inning, he screamed for a Snickers bar to satisfy a sugar craving. He then hit a solo homer and a three-run shot to spark an 8-0 Padres victory.

"He could barely make it around the bases, he was so weak," the Padres' Tony Gwynn said. "Guys were just sitting on the bench looking at each other and they couldn't believe what they had just seen."

What they had seen was typical Caminiti. "If he can walk he can play. That's always been his attitude," his father, Lee, said. Indeed, when Caminiti

"If he can walk he can play. That's always been his attitude."

30

y motto has always been if you can get on the field in any way, you've got a chance to do something."
—*Ken Caminiti, San Diego Padres*

was in high school, a broken collarbone kept him sidelined for only 10 days.

The Houston Astros included him in a 12-player trade with San Diego on December 28, 1994, fearing that his punishing style might lead to a rapid decline. But since joining the Padres, Caminiti has produced his three best seasons.

He still takes physical risks, but not the way he did earlier in his career, when he was addicted to alcohol and pain-killers. Caminiti became a different player after he underwent rehabilitation in Houston in October 1993.

"It's no coincidence that I made the All-Star team for the first time the year I quit drinking and taking painkillers and that I've had two even better years since then," he said in September 1996.

He finished that season with a .326 batting average, 40 homers and 130 RBIs, becoming only the fourth unanimous selection in the 67-year history of the National League MVP award. What made Caminiti's season even more remarkable was his ability to produce at such a high level despite injuries to his back, hamstring, groin and shoulder—not to mention the food poisoning he suffered in Mexico.

His shoulder problem was the most serious.

> *"I'm going to come back sooner than they think."*

Caminiti could barely raise his left (non-throwing) arm. Reaching for high line drives was difficult; hitting high pitches, almost impossible. Caminiti required major surgery when the season ended, but vowed, "I'm going to come back sooner than they think." Sure enough, he was in the 1997 Opening Day lineup, and produced another big year.

Just as in his MVP season, Caminiti had a monster second half. He also won his third straight Gold Glove award, the longest streak by a National League third baseman since Mike Schmidt won nine straight from '76 to '84.

"He's better than Brooks Robinson," said Padres hitting coach Merv Rettenmund, a former teammate of the Orioles' Hall of Famer. "He moves better than Brooks, and he has the stronger arm."

That's Caminiti—strong arm, strong body, strong constitution.

His teammates jokingly yelled for Snickers and IVs after he hit his two homers in Mexico, but few were under the illusion that they could have matched his feat.

"Cammy had an 'S' under his uniform," pitcher Bob Tewksbury said.

It was an 'S' that stayed there thoughout the '96 season, even with the pain in his shoulder and his other physical problems.

"If I can get to the park," Caminiti said, "I'm going to play."

Ken Caminiti/3B — San Diego Padres

	1997	CAREER
POS	3B	3B
B	S	S
G	137	1374
AVG	.290	.275
AB	486	4999
H	141	1374
2B	28	278
3B	0	15
HR	26	167
RBI	90	759
R	92	684
SB	11	73
BB	80	525
SO	118	875

Roger Clemens

PITCHER—TORONTO BLUE JAYS

R oger Clemens loves his four children. Loves them so much that he moved to the city where he thought they would be happiest. Loves them so much that he just had to win another Cy Young Award. "I got one for Koby and Kory, I got one for Kacy, and I needed one for Kody," Clemens said after becoming the first American League pitcher to win four Cy Youngs. "It kind of takes the pressure off dad a bit."

Clemens, the fifth of sixth children born to Bess Clemens, grew up without a father—his parents split when he was five and his stepfather died when he was nine.

So profound was his sense of loss that he vowed to become a devoted father. One reason he signed with the Toronto Blue Jays before the 1997 season was the team's policy of allowing players to bring their children onto the field before games.

Clemens' family history also shaped his baseball career. His work ethic and competitive fire are matched by few others, and Clemens said he acquired those qualities watching his mother work three jobs to provide for her children.

Evidently, Bess Clemens set quite an example: Clemens, 35, went six years between Cy Youngs, matching Gaylord Perry for the largest gap since the inception of the award in 1956. The 11-year span between his first and last Cy Youngs is the longest ever.

It takes a special drive to recapture such excel-

"He throws fastballs on the corner, fastballs down and in, forkballs. He's the best pitcher in the league."

Ialways had to overcome doubts others had. But I've made myself thrive on that."
—*Roger Clemens, Toronto Blue Jays*

lence. The Boston Red Sox thought Clemens was in decline after he went 40-39 over four seasons. Clemens left for Toronto with something to prove, and he revived his career.

He opened the 1997 season 11-0, then became the first American League pitcher in 52 years to lead his league in wins (21), earned-run average (2.05) and strikeouts (292).

This was the Rocket of old, not some fading legend.

Clemens earned his 200th career victory at Yankee Stadium on May 21, scooping up a handful of dirt as a keepsake. New York shortstop Derek Jeter called it "the best pitching performance I've ever seen."

Less than two months later, Clemens struck out 16 in his return to Boston's Fenway Park. His old friend, Red Sox first baseman Mo Vaughn, called him "an awesome presence on the mound."

"He's so tough," said the Texas Rangers' Juan Gonzalez, another of the game's most feared sluggers. "He throws fastballs on the corner, fastballs down and in, forkballs. He's the best pitcher in the league."

Clemens finished with his most victories since 1990 and established a career-high in strikeouts. It certainly was not his fault that the Blue Jays were a disappointing 76-86.

"The first game he pitched in Toronto was the day after Opening Day and it was like a playoff atmosphere," Blue Jays general manager Gord Ash said.

"I look at players who get other players excited. You have Wayne Gretzky in hockey. Obviously, you have Michael Jordan in basketball. Roger has that aura about him."

When you think of Clemens, you think of strikeouts, you think of intimidation, you think of a hulking, towering presence on the mound. Still, not even the Rocket blasted off right away.

Clemens was an All-State high-school pitcher in Houston, and the New York Mets drafted him out of San Jacinto Junior College in 1981. But the money for a 12th-round pick was low, and Clemens did not sign.

Instead, he spent two years at the University of Texas, winning the final game of the 1983 College World Series. Even then, scouts weren't totally convinced he would succeed. In his second crack at the draft, Clemens lasted until the 19th pick of the first round.

When you think of Clemens, you think of strikeouts...
you think of a hulking, towering presence on the mound.

"When I was coming up, nobody said I was a can't-lose prospect. They doubted my ability. I always had to overcome doubts others had. But I've made myself thrive on that."

And thrive he has, becoming the preeminent strikeout pitcher of his generation. In one 1986 game, Clemens struck out 20 to set the record for most strikeouts in a nine-inning game. He matched that feat 10 years later, again without walking a batter.

Strikeouts clearly are important to Clemens—he started each of his children's name with a "K," the letter used to indicate a strikeout on a baseball score-card. But he is not simply a 6-foot-4, 230-pound power pitcher.

As Clemens himself puts it, "I was a pitcher long before I got the power." He no longer throws as many breaking pitches—they put too much strain on his arm. Instead, he relies on pinpoint control of his fast-ball and forkball.

The question now is how long Clemens can sus-

tain it. His Blue Jays contract runs through 1999, but Clemens has talked about pitching until he is 45. He's such a warrior—and such a hard worker—that it might be possible.

He has won strikeout titles, ERA titles, even a Most Valuable Player award, but what Clemens wants now is a World Championship. He was one strike away with the 1986 Red Sox, but he hasn't returned to the World Series since.

Whether he earns a championship ring or wins a record fifth Cy Young, Clemens' final destination seems clear. He is almost certain to be elected to the Hall of Fame, and is already musing about a family vacation to Cooperstown, New York.

"It would be unbelievable," Clemens said. "Hopefully one day I can take the kids in there, turn

them loose and let them see what their dad did for 15 or 20 years."

He never had the chance to please his father. But he will please his kids.

Roger Clemens/RHP—Toronto Blue Jays

	1997	CAREER
W	21	213
L	7	118
PCT	.750	.644
G	34	417
SV	0	0
IP	264.0	3040.0
H	204	2563
R	65	1110
ER	60	1003
BB	68	924
SO	292	2882
ERA	2.05	2.97

I always wanted to be the type of pitcher who pitched every game like it was his last."
—*David Cone, New York Yankees*

David Cone

PITCHER—NEW YORK YANKEES

He's known as a "hired gun," a pitcher who moves from city to city, trying to provide the final piece of a championship puzzle. Funny thing about David Cone, though. In many ways, he's the ultimate team player.

He embraces big-game responsibility. He accepts blame for his defeats. And in his three seasons with the New York Yankees, he has sacrificed himself physically, emerging as an inspiration to his teammates.

"I always wanted to be the type of pitcher who pitched every game like it was his last," Cone once said. Time and time again over the past 12 seasons, he has done it.

He hasn't always been successful—he lost the lead in Game 5 of the 1995 Division Series against Seattle, and a shoulder injury prevented him from making his second start in the '97 Division Series against Cleveland.

Still, the enduring image of Cone is from '96, when he made a startling comeback from a career-threatening aneurysm in his right shoulder to lead the Yankees to their first world championship in 18 years.

He no longer was the fresh-faced kid who fell into a New York lifestyle during his days with the Mets. Nor was he the baseball gypsy who had been traded four times and changed teams twice as a free agent.

That season, Cone became something more.

His comeback began less than four months after

He has sacrificed himself physically, emerging as an inspiration to his teammates.

League record with a 19-strikeout game in '91. He started the World Series clincher for Toronto in '92. He won a Cy Young Award with Kansas City in '94.

Cone enjoys pressure, even invites it. He spent a turbulent 5½ years with the Mets—"I made a lot of mistakes," he said, "both on and off the field." But the second time he was a free agent, he re-signed with the Yankees.

"There's no place I'd rather be than right here, right now, pitching big games down the stretch for the Yankees.

"You hear a lot of athletes who say they are motivated by fear of failure. I couldn't disagree more. To me, it's an opportunity. This is what we live and play for."

he underwent surgery to remove the aneurysm. Cone threw seven hitless innings against the Athletics in his return. The Yankees held off Baltimore for the division title, then reached the World Series.

They trailed the Atlanta Braves, two games to none, when Cone took the mound for Game 3. The series had moved to Atlanta; the odds against the Yankees were enormous. But Cone began their turnaround, pitching six innings for a 5-2 victory.

"It's mind-boggling to put all of that in perspective," he said afterward. "Lying in the hospital bed, I knew the World Series was the farthest thing from my mind."

It was the defining moment of a career filled with memorable achievements. Cone tied a National

*"This is what we live
and play for."*

Which isn't to say that Cone is all work and no fun. He has his irreverent side—he grew up idolizing Oscar Madison, the sportswriter from the *Odd Couple*. During the '88 playoffs, he even wrote his own column for a New York tabloid. He took it too far, insulting several Dodgers—then beat them to force a Game 7.

In '90, he argued with umpires while two runs scored—"I think that night I was incoherent," Cone said. And in '92, he used a magazine as a skateboard and took a mad spin down the airplane aisle as his first flight with the Blue Jays landed.

Now 35, Cone has matured. He was so distraught over the outcome of the '95 Division Series, he secluded himself in his Manhattan apartment for two weeks, thinking about what might have been.

He had thrown nearly 240 innings that season, and tired in the decisive game. His wild pitch in the eighth forced in the tying run. Randy Johnson relieved in the ninth on one day's rest. The Mariners won, 6-5, in 11 innings to end the Yankees' season.

"Randy didn't care if he pitched another game and neither did I."

He wants the ball. He always wants the ball. It doesn't matter if Cone is pitching for the Mets or the Yankees, the Royals or the Blue Jays. The hired gun is a team player.

David Cone/RHP — New York Yankees

	1997	CAREER
W	12	148
L	6	86
PCT	.667	.632
G	29	328.0
SV	0	1
IP	195	2189.0
H	155	1794
R	67	838
ER	61	762
BB	86	836
SO	222	2034
ERA	2.82	3.13

Being older, I know how much I care about this game." — *Dennis Eckersley, St. Louis Cardinals*

Dennis Eckersley

PITCHER—ST. LOUIS CARDINALS

Dennis Eckersley hasn't simply enjoyed a magnificent career. He has authored an epic.

From a wild and crazy starting pitcher who once threw a no-hitter. To a sober closer who revived his career with the mighty Oakland A's of the late '80s and early '90s. And now, to a forty-something veteran trying to savor the final days of more than two decades in the Major Leagues.

How fitting that Eckersley is rejoining the Boston Red Sox on the 20th anniversary of his 20-win season in 1978.

"Being older, I know how much I care about this game... I'm so intense about it. It's been my whole life. So when it's over, it's like, 'Uh-oh.' I'm afraid. I'm afraid of the grief that will come, the pain."

Truth be told, the Eck has always been afraid, despite his cocky, flamboyant appearance. It is his fear of failure that makes him great.

He is a rarity among today's athletes, fretting when he lets down teammates, never making excuses, always taking blame. And from 1988 to '92, he was as dominant as any reliever in Major League history, transforming himself from a fading pitcher into a likely Hall of Famer.

Eckersley averaged 44 saves per season during that period, with nearly 10 times as many strikeouts (378) as walks (38).

In 1990, he posted a 0.61 earned-run average, the lowest in Major League history for a pitcher who worked at least 25 innings. And in 1992, he won both

He is a rarity among today's atheletes...never making excuses, always taking the blame.

45

the American League Cy Young and Most Valuable Player awards.

No one could have predicted that Eckersley's career would take such a spectacular turn after the Chicago Cubs traded him to Oakland in April 1987. But Eckersley had undergone alcohol rehabilitation that off-season, and Tony La Russa, his manager in Oakland and later in St. Louis, made him a closer.

Neither Eckersley nor La Russa regretted it: The A's proceeded to win four division titles, three American League championships and one World Series.

"He has always been a warrior on the mound. Always," La Russa said. "When he was young and crazy. When he was in Oakland, winning the Cy Young and MVP.

"And now I see him in his 40s, and it's the same. I've never seen him take the mound and not be ready for the competition. His heart is beating. The fire in his belly is just the way it was when he was a rookie."

His competitiveness sometimes got him into trouble—Eckersley would irritate opponents by pumping his fist and pointing in celebration of saves. But he was so masterful at his peak—so dominant with his stuff, so pinpoint with his control — that no one wanted to face him.

Even now, at 43, Eckersley is still effective: Excluding the strike-shortened '94 and '95 seasons, he has earned 30 or more saves every year since becoming a closer.

That's quite an accomplishment, consid-

"He has always been a warrior on the mound. Always."

*He was so dominant with his
stuff, so pinpoint with his control,
that no one wanted to face him.*

ering that late-inning specialists work under immense pressure and scrutiny. Even Eckersley has had his share of disappointment.

He endured the Kirk Gibson homer in the '88 World Series. A shocking loss to Cincinnati in the '90 World Series. The Roberto Alomar homer in the '92 American League playoffs.

After each of those crushing defeats, Eckersley stood at his locker, answering every reporter's question, refusing to criticize anyone but himself.

"I wish I could tell you my arm was hanging, I had no velocity, some excuse," he said after the Alomar

homer in '92. "But you've got to take it like a man."

He always does, but he's still not very comfortable with defeat.

"The older you get, the harder failures become . . . It's almost like I think the world is thinking, 'Look at what he did.' I know they're not, but I can't be any other way."

With his long hair and deep suntan, Eckersley looks like an aging beach bum. His appearance belies his tense approach, his fierce will to succeed.

LaRussa compares him to one of the game's all-time competitors.

"This," the manager said, "is Pete Rose sliding headfirst."

Dennis Eckersley/RHP—Boston Red Sox

	1997	CAREER
W	1	193
L	5	170
PCT	.167	.532
G	57	1021
SV	36	389
IP	53.0	3246.0
H	49	3030
R	24	1361
ER	23	1257
BB	8	730
SO	45	2379
ERA	3.91	3.49

I love the game too much not to give everything to it." —*Andres Galarraga, Colorado Rockies*

Andres Galarraga

FIRST BASE—COLORADO ROCKIES

In 1992, it didn't seem possible that Andres Galarraga would win a batting title, become a home-run king and lead the National League in RBIs in back-to-back seasons.

In 1992, in fact, it appeared that Galarraga's career might be over.

"He was as low as you can go," said Colorado Rockies manager Don Baylor. "Everyone talked about how he had lost it, that all his skills were gone, and after a while he believed it."

Galarraga had batted .219 the previous season for Montreal, and was at .189 on July 19 after getting traded to St. Louis. At the All-Star break, he had fewer homers than the player the Cardinals had traded for him—pitcher Ken Hill.

It was the year his father, Francisco, died of stomach cancer. The year he broke his wrist in the second game of the season. The year he considered quitting, even though he was only 31.

"I never told anybody, not the media, not my teammates, nobody, but I thought about going home, giving up . . . I couldn't do anything.

"I kept telling people, 'Yeah, I know I can play this game, and I know I can still hit,' but I didn't know really. And then I just started letting everything bother me."

Enter Baylor. Then the St. Louis hitting coach, the former Major League slugger advised Galarraga to open his batting stance and hit to the opposite field. Simple suggestions, perhaps. But

He made one of the most amazing turnarounds in Major League history.

49

they helped revive Galarraga's career.

At the end of that season, Baylor became the manager of the expansion Rockies, and urged general manager Bob Gebhard to sign Galarraga. Gebhard went ahead, knowing he couldn't afford a better player, anyway.

And with that, the Rockies' first star was born.

The 6-foot-3, 235-pound Galarraga is nicknamed "The Big Cat" for his agility at first base. But obviously, the two-time Gold Glove winner is more than a defensive specialist.

In his first season, Galarraga became the first Venezuelan and first expansion player to win a batting title. His .370 average was the highest by a right-handed hitter since Joe DiMaggio in 1939.

Galarraga then produced back-to-back 30-homer seasons in the strike-shortened '94 and '95 campaigns—and he posted back-to-back 40-homer

seasons in both the '96 and '97.

He batted over .300 in both of those seasons, while driving in 150 runs the first year and 140 the next. The 150 RBIs were the most by a National League player in 34 years (Tommy Davis had 153 in 1962).

Galarraga benefited from playing at hitter-friendly Coors Field—his batting average over the past five seasons was nearly 70 points higher at home than on the road.

But the Atlanta Braves were so impressed, they signed him to a three-year contract at the end of the '97 season, knowing that Galarraga would be 39 when the deal expired.

Not a bad comeback for a player who appeared so washed-up in '92 that he was bypassed by the team he wanted to join, the Florida Marlins, in favor of a Japanese League player .

Florida GM David Dombrowski knew Galarraga from their days in Montreal, but chose Orestes Destrade to play first base. Destrade lasted just two seasons, and now works in the front office for the expansion Tampa Bay Devil Rays.

Still, it was hard to fault Dombrowski's decision—Galarraga had led the National League in strikeouts three straight seasons, then lost his stroke when the Expos told him to lower his hands on the bat and pull the ball more.

Baylor took him back to basics in St. Louis, throwing him balls underhanded, making him hit off a tee. Galarraga recalls the experience as "embarrassing" and "humiliating." But it helped make him the hitter he is today.

Off the field, Galarraga is known for his infectious smile, his engaging personality, his work with youth charities. He made one of the most amazing turnarounds in Major League history.

And it couldn't have happened to a nicer guy.

Andres Galarraga/1B—Atlanta Braves

	1997	CAREER
POS	1B	1B
B	R	R
G	154	1621
AVG	.318	.288
AB	600	6074
H	191	1752
2B	31	337
3B	3	29
HR	41	288
RBI	140	1051
R	120	908
SB	15	114
BB	54	404
SO	141	1469

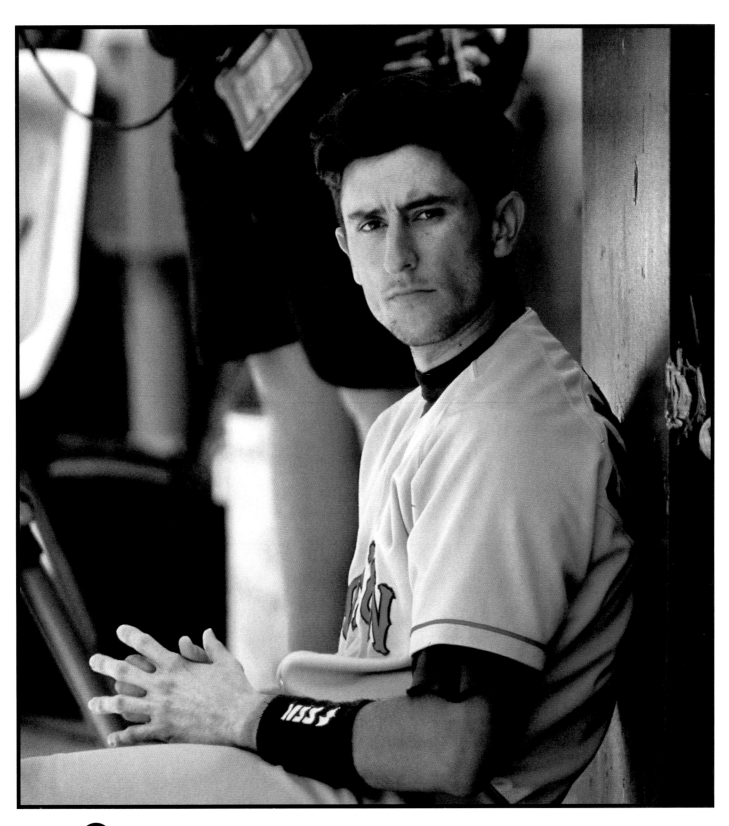

obody knows the whole game, nobody ever will." — *Nomar Garciaparra, Boston Red Sox*

Nomar Garciaparra

SHORTSTOP—BOSTON RED SOX

Toward the end of last season, Nomar Garciappara would warn reporters, "no questions about statistics." Even though he was only a rookie, he knew that baseball success isn't measured simply by numbers.

Garciaparra, the precocious Boston Red Sox shortstop, plays with a style and elegance that sets him apart not just from other young players, but veterans, too.

At shortstop, he'll glide deep into the hole, stab a sharply hit grounder, then throw out an opponent on the run. At the plate, he'll uncoil his 6-foot, 167-pound body and deliver a clutch double or game-winning homer.

Garciaparra, 24, was a unanimous choice last season as American League Rookie of the Year. And yes, his statistics were impossible to ignore.

His 98 RBIs were the most ever by a leadoff man. His 30-game hitting streak was an AL rookie record. His league-high 209 hits represented the fifth highest rookie total in Major League history.

"The best-looking shortstop we've ever seen around here," former Red Sox infielder Johnny Pesky said. "Joe Cronin couldn't field or throw with this guy. The closest is probably Luis Aparicio, but this kid's a better hitter.

"He can run. He has good baseball instincts. I'm telling you, if he'd come along in my era, I'd be sitting on the pine. You could almost classify him as the perfect player."

Strong words, considering that Pesky was a .307

"*You could almost classify him as the perfect player.*"

It is that humility that makes the southern California native so popular in the Red Sox clubhouse, a place he threatened to divide when he won the shortstop job in spring training, forcing the move of John Valentin to second base.

Garciaparra plays with a rare intelligence—he scored more than 1200 on his college-entrance exam and recorded close to a 4.0 grade-point average at his Catholic boys' high school. He also plays in complete control of his wiry body.

Red Sox first baseman Mo Vaughn calls Garciaparra "Spiderman." Pitcher Butch Henry said he's built "like a coiled spring." Third baseman Tim Naehring said, "he brings an aspect to the game we haven't had since I've been here."

Indeed, Garciaparra's game is almost as unusual as his name—Anthony Nomar Garciaparra. He is known by his middle name, which is his father's name, Ramon, spelled backwards.

"My wife thought I was crazy," Ramon said. "She said to me, 'You're not really going to name him Nomar, are you? Why are you doing that?' And I just told here, 'You wait, one day he's going to make that name famous.'"

Sure enough, it happened. When other kids went to the beach, Nomar preferred to have his father hit grounders to him. They began the routine when he was five. Ramon, a native of Guadalajara, Mexico, had Nomar wear soccer shinguards, so he wouldn't be scared to attack hard-hit balls.

lifetime hitter who missed three of his prime years due to World War II, and Cronin and Aparicio are Hall of Famers.

Garciaparra isn't in that class yet, but his first full season was so breathtaking, it left Red Sox fans yearning for more. He batted .306 with 44 doubles, a league-high 11 triples and 30 homers. He scored 122 runs, and even stole 22 bases.

What is there to improve?

"Everything," Garciaparra said. "I'm not really satisfied with anything. There's room for improvement in everything, defensively and offensively. Nobody knows the whole game, nobody ever will."

> *He plays in complete control of his wiry body.*
> *He's built "like a coiled spring."*

Garciaparra was an All-American at Georgia Tech, a 1992 U.S. Olympian and the 12th overall pick in the '94 draft. He went on to become Boston's first Rookie of the Year since Fred Lynn in 1975, but he isn't about to grow content.

"He wants to learn the game and be a great player," Red Sox general manager Dan Duquette said. "[Ted] Williams was obsessive in the way he approached the game. Yaz was. [Jim] Rice was. Cal Ripken's the same way."

And so the Red Sox torch is passed. Williams to Yastrzemski to Lynn and Rice, and on to Garciaparra.

Nomar Garciaparra/SS—Boston Red Sox

	1997	CAREER
POS	SS	SS
B	R	R
G	153	177
AVG	.306	.298
AB	684	771
H	209	230
2B	44	46
3B	11	14
HR	30	34
RBI	98	114
R	122	133
SB	22	27
BB	35	39
SO	92	106

I know what I'm doing. As far as pitching goes, I'm as good as anyone." — *Tom Glavine, Atlanta Braves*

Tom Glavine

PITCHER—ATLANTA BRAVES

Baseball isn't only a game for the biggest, strongest and fastest. Tom Glavine is one of the sport's subtle heroes, a pitcher who doesn't dominate so much as deceive.

"I know I don't have the best fastball on the staff. I know I don't have the best breaking ball . . . but I know what I'm doing. As far as pitching goes, I'm as good as anyone."

Glavine, 32, proved that when he posted three straight 20-win seasons for the Atlanta Braves from 1991 to 1993, proved it when he pitched the Game 6 clincher in the '95 World Series.

Still, many fans would probably be surprised to learn that he's the winningest left-hander in the Majors over the past decade. He doesn't throw as hard as Randy Johnson. Heck, he's not even the best pitcher on his own team.

As Glavine put it, "No one walks away thinking I was awesome." But like his more celebrated team-mate Greg Maddux, he is a master of the lost art of pitching—witness his 1991 National League Cy Young Award.

Glavine doesn't overpower hitters with fastballs; he disrupts them with changeups and sinkers. He doesn't try to intimidate by throwing inside; he paints the outside corner.

At 6-foot-1, 185 pounds, Glavine is from the same physical mold as Hall of Fame left-handers Warren Spahn and Whitey Ford. Yet, even his slight build is a deception. Few pitchers possess his mental toughness.

He doesn't try to intimidate by throwing inside; he paints the outside corner.

"He sets the standard for
this staff in terms of consistency
and competitiveness."

"There is nobody in baseball who works harder than he does. Nobody," said his teammate Greg Maddux. "You see a lot of guys in this game who won't do the work necessary to get the most out of their abilities. No one will ever say that of Tom Glavine."

"If you're talking about someone being the leader of our staff, then that has to be Tom. He sets the standard for this staff in terms of consistency and competitiveness. He's the best competitor I've ever played with."

The Braves first saw that early in Glavine's career, before they made their six straight Post Season appearances and became known as the Team of the '90s.

In 1988, Glavine's first full season, they finished 54-106. Glavine was 22 then. The Braves had rushed him to the Majors. And with a poor defense behind him, he led the National League with 17 losses.

"It's remarkable that anyone, even a pitcher with 10 or 15 years of experience, could go through what he did and not quit," said Bruce Dal Canton, the Braves' pitching coach at the time. "That, more than anything, tells you about his makeup."

Glavine grew up in blue-collar Billerica, Massachusetts, the son of a construction-business owner. He followed an older brother into sports, and became proficient not just in baseball, but in hockey.

As a high-school senior, he was considered the best hockey prospect in the Boston area, ahead of future NHL stars Tom Barrasso and Kevin Stevens. Two professional teams drafted him—the Braves and the Los Angeles Kings.

Glavine also had a scholarship offer from the University of Lowell, a Division II hockey power that would have allowed him to play both sports. But

he chose the Braves, almost out of destiny.

Glavine's father, Fred, had been a big fan of Spahn and the old Boston Braves. He even encouraged his son to pitch like the crafty left-hander, who won 363 games from 1942 to 1965.

And a modern-day Spahn was born.

Glavine was only 31-37 after his first three seasons, but since September 1990, he has won nearly 70 percent of his decisions, started two All-Star Games and pitched in four World Series.

His signature performance came in the '95 Series clincher, when he held the powerful Cleveland Indians to one hit over eight innings in a 1-0 victory. His career 1.75 ERA in the Series is tied for sixth on the all-time list.

He isn't the biggest, strongest or fastest, but NL Cy Young winner Pedro Martinez says Glavine is the pitcher he watches most closely. Those who know the game appreciate the subtle heroes, appreciate the Tom Glavines.

Tom Glavine/LHP — Atlanta Braves

	1997	CAREER
W	14	153
L	7	99
PCT	.667	.607
G	33	331
SV	0	0
IP	240.0	2196.1
H	197	2068
R	86	928
ER	79	830
BB	79	743
SO	152	1364
ERA	2.96	3.40

I want my people to be proud of me. They need somebody." — *Juan Gonzalez, Texas Rangers*

Juan Gonzalez

OUTFIELD—TEXAS RANGERS

"Igor" might be the perfect nickname for a slugger, but inside Juan Gonzalez's powerful body is a soft heart.

Every winter, he returns home to Vega Baja, Puerto Rico, where he pays for everything from Little Leagues to drug prescriptions to funerals.

"I have things to do outside the lines," the Texas Rangers outfielder said. "I want my people to be proud of me. They need somebody."

Gonzalez, 28, has never forgotten his roots, but in recent seasons he has achieved greater maturity as both a player and a person.

A three-day church retreat before the 1996 season persuaded him to shift his priorities. Gonzalez now ranks baseball No. 3, behind God and family. And he's an even better player than before.

He was a two-time home-run king by the age of 24, but he didn't work at his defense, didn't always hustle or play through pain. Some described him as moody and selfish. Off the field, he went through three divorces.

The difference now is evident.

"I see it in his body language," Texas manager Johnny Oates said. "It's fun to watch him play. Juan seems to be enjoying himself. I don't think there's been any change in effort; he just seems to be enjoying himself more."

Gonzalez certainly enjoyed the '96 season, the first after his spiritual awakening. Despite missing 28 games with various injuries, he batted .314 with

"It's fun to watch him play. Juan seems to be enjoying himself."

47 homers and 147 RBIs.

His average of 1.07 RBIs per game was the highest in the Majors in more than half a century. And he joined Roberto Clemente, Orlando Cepeda and Willie Hernandez as the only natives of Puerto Rico to win a Most Valuable Player Award.

Gonzalez's numbers declined slightly in '97, but he again showed a desire to play every day, appearing in 133 of the Rangers' final 138 games after missing the first 24 with a thumb problem.

"We all come to a crossroads in our lives, a place in the road where you can go one way or the other," said Sandy Johnson, the scout who signed Gonzalez at the age of 16 in 1986.

"Juan was at that crossroads, and he went the right way. I can't say it was this or that—sometimes a light just goes off, and you find the path you should be on."

Now that he's on that path, it's exciting to consider what he might accomplish. In seven full seasons, he has averaged 36 homers and 110 RBIs. If he stays healthy—always a question for the 6-foot-3, 220-pound Gonzalez—he could hit 500 homers.

Of all his power displays, the most memorable probably came in the '96 Division Series against the New York Yankees. Gonzalez hit five home runs in

> [
> *If he stays healthy,*
> *he could hit 500 homers.*
>]

four games, tying the record for the most in a single Post Season series.

Yankees manager Joe Torre ate in the same restaurant as Gonzalez in Texas the day before Game 3. "I didn't know whether to have him pick up the check or poison his food," Torre said.

Gonzalez's playoff heroics and subsequent MVP Award only reinforced his standing as the biggest baseball hero in Puerto Rico since the late Clemente.

"He left some footprints that can never be filled, that can never be surpassed, because he is one of the greatest players in the history of the game . . . and off the field, one of the greatest human beings," Gonzalez said.

Gonzalez, though, is trying to fulfill Clemente's legacy. He purchases tickets for underprivileged chil-

dren in Texas, contributes to literacy programs and pays for the construction of baseball fields. But it is Puerto Rico that he holds dearest.

His hometown, Vega Baja, is located 25 miles west of San Juan. Gonzalez is so popular there that some think he might run for mayor after he leaves baseball. "When I retire, I want to come back and help these people," he said.

He always had that sense of community, and now he has the maturity to make an even greater impact.

God, family and baseball—Juan Gonzalez's personal Triple Crown.

Juan Gonzalez/OF — Texas Rangers

	1997	CAREER
POS	OF	OF
B	R	R
G	133	950
AVG	.296	.285
AB	533	3663
H	158	1045
2B	24	196
3B	3	16
HR	42	256
RBI	131	790
R	87	567
SB	0	16
BB	33	247
SO	107	716

As long as I can look in the mirror and know I've done everything I could for my team, that's all I care about." — *Ken Griffey, Seattle Mariners*

Ken Griffey Jr.

OUTFIELD—SEATTLE MARINERS

He is baseball's answer to Michael Jordan, capable of hitting a majestic homer, making a breathtaking catch, leaping a tall building in a single bound.

Maybe Ken Griffey Jr. should star in his own movie—"Base Jam" perhaps? All those kids around the country wearing his No. 24 Seattle jersey would love it.

Part of Griffey's appeal is that he often looks like a big kid, wearing his cap backward, flashing a winning smile. The other part is the electricity he creates on a baseball field.

"He plays the game the way it should be played—he goes out and has fun," Hall of Famer Frank Robinson said. "You can see it. You can feel it in the stands watching him, every time he walks up to the plate."

Why shouldn't Griffey radiate confidence? He is the son of former Major Leaguer Ken Griffey Sr., who batted .296 over 19 seasons. And like Barry Bonds, he is an even better player than his father.

He reached the Major Leagues at 19, made his first All-Star team at 20, produced his first 100-RBI season at 21. He has won eight straight Gold Gloves in center field at 28, and he's a .302 lifetime hitter with 294 home runs.

And to think that his career statistics might be even better if he had not missed nearly a month in 1996 with a broken bone in his right hand, and nearly three months in '95 with a fractured left wrist.

"We've got Edgar Martinez, the best hitter in the

"He plays the game the way it should be played — he goes out and has fun...."

"He's one of the most exciting and inspiring baseball players this league has ever seen."

to the first of their five NBA titles. Griffey, a nine-year veteran, lifted the Mariners to the Post-Season in '95 and '97, but unlike his father, he has yet to win a World Series.

"There are no bragging rights," Junior said the night he was named MVP. "My dad still has the (replica World Series) trophy at the house. He has the flags hanging off the mantle and I don't. That's what our family plays baseball for, those flags, and that's what I want."

Griffey and his father made Major League history when they played alongside each other for the Mariners in 1990 and 1991—Junior in center, Senior in left. They remain close, speaking as often as four or five times a week. And yet, so much is different now.

The diligent son has evolved into a dedicated father—Griffey, married with two children, is a homebody who enjoys playing cards, video games and dominoes.

And the teenage phenom has evolved into a community-minded superstar—Griffey takes a personal involvement in his two favorite charities, the Boys & Girls Club and Make-a-Wish Foundation.

He annually sponsors Christmas dinners for 350 Seattle Boys & Girls Club members, even accompanies them on trips to Disneyland. In 1996, he was recognized as the professional athlete who gave the most personal time to Make-a-Wish.

And then there is Griffey the player.

"What Junior is going to do throughout the course of his career is going to well overtake anything I've ever done," said Barry Bonds, Griffey's principal rival for the title, "Best Player in Baseball."

"Junior started in the game three years younger than I was when I came into the league. Junior is going to take the game to another level that I don't think anyone is going to be able to catch up to.

league. Dan Wilson, the best catcher. Randy Johnson, the best pitcher," Seattle shortstop Alex Rodriguez said. "Then you look over in the corner and there's the big man. The big man can do it all."

The big man earned his first Most Valuable Player Award last season, hitting 56 homers, the eighth highest total in Major League history, and driving in 147 runs, the sixth highest total in the last 48 years. But what he craves most is a World Series ring.

It took Jordan six years to lead the Chicago Bulls

Griffey is baseball's answer to Michael Jordan.

Griffey's popularity keeps increasing—he has led the Majors in All-Star votes three of the past four seasons. However, he seems to be growing weary of the expectations surrounding him.

"All my life in professional baseball, people said, 'He could be better,'" Griffey said. "There's always a 'but' after everything I've done. You grow tired of somebody saying, 'He hit 49, but he didn't do something else.' It's not fair.'"

"Sure, someday there will be some other kid who comes along and may be as good as Junior. But Junior will surpass me throughout his career, by a lot. Not by a little. By a lot."

That's saying something, considering Bonds is a three-time MVP, but such is the respect Griffey commands throughout baseball. He is admired by players, adored by fans, feared by opposing managers.

"The strategy is to throw it over the plate and hide my eyes," former Kansas City manager Bob Boone once said. "From now on, I'm going to go into the bathroom when he bats. Tell me what happens."

Griffey holds the record for most home runs by the end of April (13), May (23) and June (32). He and Mark McGwire are the leading candidates to break Roger Maris' single-season record of 61.

Last season, Hall of Famer Reggie Jackson described Griffey as the "perfect guy" to overtake Maris, noting that he would receive far more public support than Maris and Hank Aaron did while chasing Babe Ruth's home-run records.

> *He is admired by players,*
> *adored by fans, feared by*
> *opposing managers.*

True, but such is the magic of Ken Griffey Jr. He's not merely capable of hitting a majestic homer, making a breathtaking catch, leaping a tall building in a single bound. He's capable of more.

Ken Griffey/OF — Seattle Mariners

	1997	CAREER
POS	OF	OF
B	L	L
G	157	1214
AVG	.304	.302
AB	608	4593
H	185	1389
2B	34	261
3B	3	24
HR	56	294
RBI	147	872
R	125	820
SB	15	123
BB	76	580
SO	121	755

It's more than just having natural talent. It's being smart, and doing your homework and paying attention to detail and then going up and executing." — *Tony Gwynn, San Diego Padres*

Tony Gwynn

OUTFIELD—SAN DIEGO PADRES

Ty Cobb. Honus Wagner. Tony Gwynn. Those are the only players in Major League history to win eight batting titles. And Gwynn, after tying Wagner's National League record last season, has a chance to match Cobb's all-time mark of 12.

Impossible? Well, the San Diego outfielder is four titles short, and almost 38 years old. Then again, he has won four straight titles since turning 34, and is coming off the best season of his 16-year career.

"I might be just reaching my prime," Gwynn said.

That's no idle boast—Gwynn established career highs in hits, doubles, RBIs and home runs last season, and erased an eight-point deficit in the final two weeks to overtake Larry Walker for his eighth batting title.

Cobb, Wagner, Gwynn.

Exclusive company, but nothing unusual for a left-handed hitter who has gone three consecutive starts without a hit only *once* in his career.

Sports Illustrated proclaimed Gwynn "The Best Hitter Since Ted Williams" in a cover story last July. *The Sporting News* put him on its cover with Stan Musial the same week, labeling them, "The Naturals."

For Gwynn, the recognition was overdue. If he played in a larger media market, more fans would understand that he not only is one of the game's best players, but also one of its best people.

In 1995, Gwynn won the Branch Rickey Award for community service by a Major leaguer. He is unfail-

*"The best hitter since
Ted Williams."*

ingly humble and always accessible. And he holds the game in deep respect.

Gwynn makes hitting look effortless, but no hitter works harder at his craft. He still takes two VCRs with him on the road, one to record games, the other to break down at-bats on three separate tapes.

Hour after hour, Gwynn analyzes "good" at-bats, at-bats that produced hits and swings that produced hits. He's so rarely satisfied, that he once complained to his wife, Alicia, that a 5-for-5 day was "ugly."

> *He's so rarely satisfied, that he once complained to his wife, Alicia, that a 5-for-5 day was "ugly."*

All hitters should look so terrible.

"If it doesn't bounce, Tony can hit it," Padres hitting coach Merv Rettenmund said. "I've seen him hit balls off the ground and balls eye-high. I've seen him hit balls off the plate inside and outside.

"Tony's in the top one percent of hitters who've ever played. He recognizes the pitch so early, it's like he's calling it out of the pitcher's hand."

From there, Gwynn's mechanics take over. He's a master of the "inside-out" swing, a stroke that

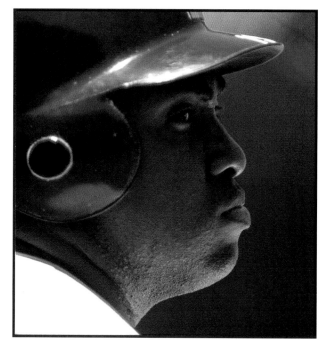

"He recognizes the pitch so early,
it's like he's calling it
out of the pitcher's hand."

his wife in elementary school and started dating her in high school. He has played his entire career in San Diego, turning down several chances to make more money with another team.

Even in the off-season, Gwynn keeps a low profile, spending his winters in Indiana, where his wife has business interests. At 5-foot-10 and 220 pounds, he probably could walk through the streets of New York City unnoticed.

Once upon a time, he was a dazzling point guard who set the all-time assists record at San Diego

enables him to shoot the ball to the opposite field. In 1993, he developed a timing mechanism with his front foot, and added power.

Gwynn is forever studying, forever learning, forever trying to improve. He has talked hitting with Williams and Musial. Rod Carew and George Brett. Wille Mays and Pete Rose.

"I've had the opportunity to sit down and talk to some of the best players who ever played the game," he said. "I've tried to pick their brains a little bit and tried to understand how they did what they did.

"I've taken a lot of different bits from a lot of different people and tried to incorporate it. Ted Williams' advice (to drive inside pitches) probably has paid the biggest dividends, but I really took a little bit from everybody."

For Gwynn, it's all a matter of repetition, a matter of routine. Like many great hitters, he is superstitious. In both his personal and professional life, he abhors change.

A native of Long Beach, California, Gwynn met

State. Nearly two decades later, he is a future Hall of Famer who has batted .350 for five straight seasons, and .300 for 15 straight.

At the end of the '92 season, Gwynn's career average was .327.

Today, it's .340.

"As good as he was in the '80s, he's gotten better," Padres manager Bruce Bochy said. "He hasn't lost any hand-eye coordination. Maybe it's fair to say he has lost a step, but he's gotten so much smarter as a hitter, knowing how they're going to pitch him, that his overall game is just better than it's ever been."

Cobb's record? Gwynn doesn't think it's within reach: "Twelve (batting titles)," he said, "that's a whole bunch." But it could happen in this age of diluted pitching, if his reflexes stay sharp and his body stays willing.

Gwynn won his first batting title during Ronald Reagan's first term. He hit .358 but finished second to Andres Galarraga in 1993. He held off Mike Piazza playing with a painful foot injury in '96.

"I'm 37 and better than I was 10 years ago," Gwynn said. "I feel good about that and don't feel bashful about saying that. I've really thought about that. The last three or four years, I've actually gotten better."

Ty Cobb. Honus Wagner. Tony Gwynn.

Tony Gwynn/OF — San Diego Padres

	1997	CAREER
POS	OF	OF
B	L	L
G	149	2095
AVG	.372	.340
AB	592	8187
H	220	2780
2B	49	460
3B	2	84
HR	17	107
RBI	119	973
R	97	1237
SB	12	308
BB	43	707
SO	28	389

There's no situation I can't get out of with a little determination and a big heart."
–*Randy Johnson, Seattle Mariners*

Randy Johnson

PITCHER—SEATTLE MARINERS

The illness strikes whenever a certain 6-foot-10 left-hander is scheduled to pitch for the Seattle Mariners.

Left-handed hitters as prominent as Wade Boggs, Rafael Palmeiro and Larry Walker succumb to the Randy Johnson Flu.

How frightening is it facing "The Big Unit" from the left side?

Just ask former Philadelphia Phillie John Kruk, who had a memorable, if futile, at-bat against Johnson in the 1993 All-Star Game.

Kruk was so terrified after Johnson fired an 0-1 pitch over his head that he waved at the next two breaking balls, eager to return to the safety of the dugout.

"For two days, I couldn't sleep thinking about that guy," Kruk said.

Facing Johnson is indeed one of the unique experiences in baseball. He stands so tall on the mound that hitters say it appears as though he could reach out and touch home plate with the ball.

Johnson's height, however, wasn't always an advantage. Pitching requires body control, and early in his career, Johnson struggled to throw strikes. He was also considered an oddity as he worked to become the tallest player in Major League history.

His first team, the Montreal Expos, would ask him to pose with another Minor Leaguer, 5-foot-1 shortstop Mel Houston. Johnson hated the extra attention. It was difficult enough trying to refine his pitching delivery.

Hitters say it appears as though he could reach out and touch home plate with the ball.

"I struggled with my height and I got tired of constantly going to Minor League cities, where I felt like I was in a three-ring circus," he said. "I felt like I was one of the acts."

He was still a raw talent when the Expos traded him and two other pitchers to the Mariners for veteran left-hander Mark Langston in May of 1989.

Johnson led the American League in walks in each of his first three full seasons with Seattle. He was 49-48 lifetime entering the '93 season.

Since then, he's 75-20—a winning percentage of almost .800.

Johnson, 34, has gone from the most unpredictable pitcher in the sport to perhaps the most predictable. When he's on the mound, the Mariners almost never lose.

Billy Connors, the former pitching coach in Seattle, recalled the difference he noticed in Johnson watching him warm up to start the 1995 All-Star Game.

"I couldn't believe the amount of strikes he was throwing," said Connors, now a Minor League pitching instructor with the New York Yankees.

"He's like Koufax and Ryan. All of a sudden they have success, and then the confidence comes. The same thing is true with Randy. He finally got some hitters out, and then it was all over."

Johnson led the Majors in strikeouts from 1992 to 1995, joining Rube Waddell, Dizzy Dean and Bob

Johnson has gone from the most unpredictable pitcher to perhaps the most predictable.

Feller as the only pitchers to win four consecutive strikeout titles.

His Cy Young Award season in '95 was one of the most dominant in recent memory. Including the playoffs, the Mariners went 27-3 in Johnson's starts.

The stakes that season were unusually high—the Mariners wanted local government officials to approve funding for a new stadium. Their dramatic playoff run energized the region. Johnson helped save baseball in Seattle.

He pitched a three-hit complete game to defeat California in a one-game playoff for the AL West title. And he struck out six pitching in relief on one day's rest in the deciding game of the Division Series against the Yankees.

Johnson made only eight starts the next season due to a back injury that eventually required surgery. But he rebounded in '97 with his first 20-win season and a career-best 2.28 ERA.

Looking back, Johnson believes the most tragic event in his life — the death of his father, Bud, on Christmas Day 1992 — proved the turning point of his career.

"That was the year my heart became a lot bigger," Johnson said. "It's a matter of maturity and it's a matter of my heart getting bigger and it's a matter of

dedicating myself to be the best."

Once, he was allergic to home plate. Now, he spreads the Randy Johnson Flu.

Randy Johnson/LHP — Seattle Mariners

	1997	CAREER
W	20	124
L	4	68
PCT	.833	.646
G	30	262
SV	0	2
IP	213.0	1734.0
H	147	1320
R	60	725
ER	54	650
BB	77	857
SO	291	2000
ERA	2.28	3.37

Chuck Knoblauch

SECOND BASE—MINNESOTA TWINS

o understand the roots of Chuck Knoblauch's success, consider a conversation that took place in 1989 between his father, Ray, and the former general manager of the Minnesota Twins, Andy MacPhail.

Knoblauch, the Twins' first-round draft pick out of Texas A&M, wanted a guarantee that he would be invited to Major League training camp in 1990.

"I went down to Houston to see the family," MacPhail recalled. "I told him, 'We'll let you earn it. If you hit .270 in our organization this summer, we'll invite you to camp.

"That's when his father Ray, a big ol' Texas guy, jumped in and said, 'No, make it .300. If he doesn't hit .300, he doesn't deserve to go to training camp.' I knew then that this was a kid with the genes of a competitor."

Knoblauch, 29, is the youngest of six children. His father is a former Minor League pitcher and high-school baseball coach. And suffice it to say, his batting average that first season was .308.

Leave it to the 5-foot-9, 169-pound Knoblauch to exceed his father's standards and everyone else's. He's a four-time All-Star at second base, but he's forever trying to improve his game. Competitive genes indeed.

"I remember being three or four years old playing Wiffle ball with my brother in the front yard," Knoblauch said. "He's seven years older than me and he's always been a big guy—he's 6-foot-5. But I would cry if we were called into supper and I was losing

He's a four-time All-Star at second base, but he's forever trying to improve his game.

You have to focus in on every at-bat and pretend the score is 0-0, even during a blowout."
— *Chuck Knoblauch, Minnesota Twins*

that Wiffle ball game. "I wanted to stay out there until I won."

All these years later, little has changed. Knoblauch still wants to be out there. In fact, he has played in 94.9 percent of the Twins' games since joining the club in 1991.

His scrappy style of play evokes memories of a young Pete Rose, and so does his offensive production. Rose began his career at second before moving to the outfield. After seven seasons, Knoblauch's statistics are comparable.

Rose, baseball's all-time hit king, batted .309 his first seven years, with 1,327 hits, 218 doubles, 69 homers, 400 RBIs and 46 stolen bases.

Knoblauch has batted five points lower with 130

> *"There's always somebody
> better than you. I think
> that's what drives me."*

fewer hits, eight fewer doubles, 26 fewer homers, nine fewer RBIs and 230 more stolen bases.

He might not be the next Rose, but he shares the same work ethic, the same burning desire to succeed.

"Two people can have the same ability and walk out on the field, one guy who does nothing and one guy who does all the work," Knoblauch said. "The guy who does all the work is going to come out on top. Every time. Not nine out of 10 times. Not 99 times out of 100, but every time. I believe that."

Believes it? Knoblauch *lives* it. Which is how he jumped from Double A to the Majors in '91, started for a World Series champion and was named American League Rookie of the Year.

Knoblauch batted .326 that Post Season, and combined with shortstop Greg Gagne to pull a veteran move in Game 7 of the World Series, "deking" Atlanta's Lonnie Smith at second and costing the Braves a run.

The Twins have yet to return to the playoffs, but Knoblauch has emerged as their best player. His play reached a new level in '95, after he enlisted a personal trainer, adopted new workout and diet regimens and dropped 10 pounds.

Knoblauch batted .333 that season and .341 the next, leading the American League with 14 triples and scoring 140 runs. His average dipped to .291 last season, but he finished second in the AL with 62 stolen bases.

"You get to every level from high school on up, and there's always somebody better than you. I think that's what drives me," Knoblauch said.

"There's somebody out there who's younger or bigger or stronger or faster, who's coming up to take away what I like to do. Somebody's always coming after you, so you'd better be ready."

Knoblauch will be. You expect him to stop?

Chuck Knoblauch/2B—Minnesota Twins

	1997	CAREER
POS	2B	2B
B	R	R
G	156	1013
AVG	.291	.304
AB	611	3939
H	178	1197
2B	26	210
3B	10	51
HR	9	43
RBI	58	391
R	117	713
SB	62	276
BB	84	513
SO	84	453

Playing shortstop for the Big Red Machine was a big thing when we were kids."
— *Barry Larkin, Cincinnati Reds*

Barry Larkin

SHORTSTOP—CINCINNATI REDS

Barry Larkin is the best athlete in his family. And that's saying something.

His oldest brother, Mike, was a star linebacker at Notre Dame. His younger brother, Byron, is the all-time leading basketball scorer at Xavier. And his youngest brother, Stephen, is a Minor Leaguer with the Cincinnati Reds.

Barry? He's a three-time Gold Glove winner, nine-time All-Star and the only shortstop in Major League history to hit 30 home runs and steal 30 bases in the same season. Try topping that, siblings.

Larkin's sister and three brothers can't, but he credits his family with helping forge his competitive spirit. The first four children were born within five years of each other. Stephen is seven years younger than Byron.

"The biggest thing I got out of growing up with my two brothers and sister—because she was competitive, too—was the willingness to put forth the effort to win.

"If you didn't win in my household, you ended up with a bloody nose, or crying or getting beat up."

Still, his brother Mike recalled that Barry never enjoyed inflicting pain. The only thing he loved to hit was a baseball, even though he became an all-state defensive back at Cincinnati's fabled Moeller High School.

The Reds took him in the second round of the 1982 draft, projecting him as their biggest hometown star since Pete Rose. Larkin instead chose to

He has emerged as a leader and perhaps the most versatile offensive shortstop ever to play the game.

And that wasn't even his MVP season.

No, Larkin won that award the previous year, after batting .315 with 15 homers, 66 RBIs and 51 steals to lift the Reds to the National League Central title. And even then, his statistics didn't reflect his full value.

Larkin plays hurt. He counsels younger Reds on off-the-field issues. He sets an example with his work ethic, and with his play.

"I've never seen him make a mental mistake on the diamond. Never," Reds pitcher Jose Rijo said. "Of course, nobody gets results every time up. Nobody hits 1.000.

"But Larkin's approach of trying to get done what has to be done—the hit-and-run, hitting the other way, jerking the ball out of the park—is as close to perfect as you're ever going to see."

Larkin and his brothers credit their father, Robert, with teaching them that proper approach. Robert played baseball himself growing up in

attend Michigan, and the Reds drafted him again in '85—with the fourth overall pick.

From that day, it took him only 14 months to reach the Major leagues, only three years to become an All-Star and just over five years to win a World Series.

"Playing shortstop for the Big Red Machine was a big thing when we were kids," Larkin said. "It's still a big deal. Just being a shortstop is a big deal."

Larkin's career has been marked by injuries—he appeared in only 73 games last season due to assorted leg problems—but he has emerged as a leader and perhaps the most versatile offensive shortstop ever to play the game.

Some shortstops hit for more power (Ernie Banks, Cal Ripken). Others displayed more speed (Maury Wills, Bert Campaneris). But Larkin's 30-30 in '96 reflected his rare combination of two of the most coveted tools in baseball.

Mississippi in the 1950s. But back then, opportunities for blacks were limited.

Robert met his wife, Shirley, in college, and became a chemist. His sons all wanted to be action heroes. But Robert taught them all the right athletic lessons, just in case none of them turned out to be Superman.

"Stay calm," Byron recalled him saying. "No matter how crazy things get, no matter how much pressure there is, *think*. I've never seen Dad flustered—by anything. He always has that logical, precise, scientific approach."

Robert and Shirley Larkin raised a college football star, a college basketball star and a likely Hall of Fame baseball player, with another potential Major Leaguer on the way.

Barry became the best of them. Barry became the hometown shortstop. Barry became an MVP.

Barry Larkin/SS—Cincinnati Reds

	1997	CAREER
POS	SS	SS
B	R	R
G	73	1401
AVG	.317	.299
AB	224	5170
H	71	1547
2B	17	271
3B	3	51
HR	4	139
RBI	20	646
R	34	862
SB	14	289
BB	47	592
SO	24	507

Kenny Lofton

OUTFIELD—CLEVELAND INDIANS

The most enduring rule of baseball is that the bases are 90 feet apart. And no one shrinks that 90 feet like Kenny Lofton.

A pitcher can dominate with his arm, a slugger with his bat, an infielder with his glove. Lofton is one of the few players who dominates with his legs.

Home to first? Lofton runs it in less than four seconds.

First to second? Lofton beats most catchers' throws.

Second to home? Lofton took that route in the 1995 American League Championship Series—on a passed ball.

He films commercials with Olympic sprinters Michael Johnson and Gail Devers. He lights up stopwatches like Randy Johnson lights up radar guns.

"He's a nine-inning nightmare," catcher John Flaherty said.

After spending 1997 with Atlanta, Lofton is back in Cleveland, where he became only the second player in American League history to lead the league in stolen bases each of his first five seasons, along with Luis Aparicio.

He is an unlikely star, a player who excelled in basketball, not baseball, at the University of Arizona. But when scouts talk about him, they invoke an old baseball axiom: Speed comes to the ballpark every day.

On offense, the left-handed hitting Lofton can score without getting a hit, reaching first on a walk,

"He's a nine-inning nightmare."

When a person is focused on one thing and one thing only, you can accomplish a lot."
— *Kenny Lofton, Cleveland Indians*

[*"He did everything fast.*
Eat fast. Sleep fast."]

in East Chicago, Indiana. He was raised by his grandmother. At first, he slept in a converted dresser drawer. But even as a youngster, he was a blur.

"He did everything fast. Eat fast. Sleep fast," recalled a cousin, Michael Lewis. "He'd finish his schoolwork first and sit there and tap his fingers."

He grew to 6 feet, 180 pounds, then went to Arizona, where he was the point guard for the No. 1-ranked team entering the 1989 NCAA tournament.

His basketball career ended in the Sweet 16, however, when he gave up the game-winning shot to UNLV's Anderson Hunt. After the game, Lofton buried his face in a towel. And, strangely enough, a star was born.

Lofton, a 17th-round draft pick, had signed with the Houston Astros after his junior year. He agreed to try professional baseball under the condition that he could finish his basketball career and earn his degree.

"He was awkward, crude," said Clark Crist, the scout who signed him. "He had a big hitch in his swing. Fly balls, he didn't take real good routes to them. He caught up to them because he was fast. But he had a tool not many

stealing second and third, then jogging home on a sacrifice fly.

On defense, he is equally adept at preventing runs, running down balls in center field so smoothly that he once earned four consecutive Gold Gloves.

No one could have predicted his ascent. Not when he comes from such humble roots. And not when he played only five baseball games in college.

"It did kind of surprise me," Lofton said. "It's hard to be recognized in this game. But when a person is focused on one thing and one thing only, you can accomplish a lot."

Lofton was a three-pound baby born into poverty

people had, a tool to build around."

The tool was speed. It enabled Lofton to skip Double A and reach the Majors by 1991. But the Astros, needing a catcher, traded Lofton and a Minor Leaguer to Cleveland for catcher Eddie Taubensee and pitcher Willie Blair.

The deal was an immediate success for the Indians, a disaster for the Astros. Lofton stole 66 bases his first season in Cleveland, then 70, 60, 54 and 75 his next four.

A .316 lifetime hitter, he tormented Seattle in the 1995 ALCS, batting .458 with four stolen bases and four runs. And he was just as devastating against Atlanta in the World Series, stealing six bases and scoring six runs.

His one season with the Braves was a disappointment—Lofton missed 34 of 35 games at mid-season

with a groin injury—but now he is back with the franchise he helped revive, the franchise that made him a star.

"It's like I was a ghost for a year," he said.

Catchers sure find him spooky. Kenny Lofton makes 90 feet disappear.

Kenny Lofton/OF — Cleveland Indians

	1997	CAREER
POS	OF	OF
B	L	L
G	122	822
AVG	.333	.316
AB	493	3314
H	164	1047
2B	20	153
3B	6	48
HR	5	44
RBI	48	309
R	90	641
SB	27	354
BB	64	371
SO	83	426

I just pitch, that's all. That's the only thing I know how to do. I don't know any other way to say it. I just pitch." — *Greg Maddux, Atlanta Braves*

Greg Maddux

PITCHER—ATLANTA BRAVES

G reg Maddux doesn't have a Hall of Fame body—
"I don't look like a baseball player. I mean, look at me," the 6-foot, 175-pound right-hander once said.

He doesn't have a Hall of Fame arm—"He's not the oooh and the aaah and the wow and the pow and the strikeout," Atlanta pitching coach Leo Mazzone said.

What makes Maddux the most dominant pitcher of his generation—the best right-hander in the past 75 years, according to *Sports Illlustrated*—is his Hall of Fame brain.

Pitching is as much a mental exercise as it is a physical challenge. And Maddux, 31, possesses one of the sharpest minds in the history of the game.

"He has the ability to read hitters after one pitch," said Jim Lefebvre, his former manager with the Chicago Cubs. "He can already see what the hitter is trying to do and use that very thing to immediately get him out."

One pitch? Sometimes, Maddux doesn't even need that much.

"He has a tremendous ability to notice things that are going on during the course of the game," said left-hander Tom Glavine, Maddux's teammate on the Braves.

"He'll notice a guy moving up in the box on him, or he can watch a guy taking warmup swings on deck and have an idea what that guy is going to look for based on his warmup swings."

Most pitchers have enough trouble solving the hitters at the plate, much less the ones on deck. But

What makes Maddux the most dominant pitcher of his generation is his Hall of Fame brain.

93

Maddux always had exceptional aptitude. His father, Dave, said that he had a great memory even as a young boy.

Still, this is not just some pitching Mozart. Maddux is forever jotting down notes on scraps of paper to remind himself of hitters' tendencies. He admits he isn't the hardest-working pitcher. But he might be the most prepared.

"The talent is not God's gift to him alone," Braves manager Bobby Cox said. "He studies the game like mad. Literally every hitter."

Combine that encyclopedic knowledge with a flawless delivery and fierce desire, and you've got the

> "He studies the game like mad.
> Literally every hitter."

only pitcher in Major League history to win four consecutive Cy Young Awards.

In an era dominated by hitting prowess, Maddux continues to redefine pitching excellence. From 1992 to '95, his ERA was 1.98, while the National League ERA was 4.00. During that period, Maddux became the first pitcher since Walter Johnson in 1918–19 to post ERAs below 1.70 in consecutive seasons, and the only pitcher besides Sandy Koufax to post ERAs below 2.40 in four straight.

"It's really hard for me to talk about the history of the game because my history goes back 10 years,"

Maddux has an encyclopedic knowledge with a flawless delivery and fierce desire....

Maddux said after winning his fourth Cy Young in 1995.

"When I hear comparisons to people who pitched in the '50s or '60s or '70s, I can't really relate to it. I didn't really watch baseball a whole lot then. I really wasn't the fan I am now. I just take it as a nice compliment and move on."

And move on he has. Maddux "slumped" in '96 (15-11, 2.72), but rebounded with another Cy Young-quality season in '97 (19-4, 2.20). It was his 10th straight season of 15 or more victories.

"If he's pitching for his life and I'm hitting for mine, he wins," eight-time National League batting champ Tony Gwynn said. "Yeah, he definitely wins."

"Monet. Matisse. Maddux"—that was the text for an advertisement by the Braves' television affiliate last season. Maddux paints with his fastball, not a brush, but the implication was clear—he, too, is an artist.

None of his five pitches is considered exceptional, but Maddux will throw any of them in any count, and he always knows exactly where each is going.

Maddux paints with his fastball...
he, too, is an artist.

"We've always been told that a pitcher without control has nothing," Cox said. "He's the perfect example of a pitcher with great control that has everything."

Indeed, Maddux's fastball tops out at only 86 mph, but he is stingy with home runs (128 in his 12-year career) and nearly as stingy with walks (92 over the past four years).

"That's why he usually pitches nine innings in two hours," the Baltimore Orioles' Brady Anderson said. "He throws about three balls a night."

And opposing hitters rarely make solid contact on his strikes.

"Guys get up there and maybe get comfortable because he's not throwing hard," Glavine said. "They may be thinking, 'He's going to throw me a fastball and I'll just sit on a fastball. I can hit the fastball.'

"But instead, maybe he throws a changeup or curve or slider and they never see the fastball they're looking for. Their approach might be right, but Greg might not pitch them that way and they end up getting themselves out."

A classic example occurred in Game 1 of the 1995 World Series—Maddux pitched a two-hit complete game, and the Cleveland Indians hit only four balls out of the infield all night.

He is such a workhorse that he led the NL in innings pitched for five straight seasons. And he is such a good fielder that he has won eight straight Gold Gloves.

Still, for all his accomplishments, Maddux is a famously unassuming sort who wears glasses off the field, and likes to relax playing Nintendo and golf. He once visited Disney World with his wife, and barely got noticed.

Ask him the secret of pitching, and he'll reply, "Locate your fastball on both sides of the plate and change speeds." That's about as expansive as he gets.

"I just pitch, that's all," Maddux said. "That's the only thing I know how to do. I don't know any other way to say it. I just pitch."

And Sinatra just sang. And Nureyev just danced.

Greg Maddux/RHP—Atlanta Braves

	1997	CAREER
W	19	184
L	4	108
PCT	.826	.630
G	33	369
SV	0	0
IP	232.2	2598.1
H	200	2302
R	58	953
ER	57	810
BB	20	609
SO	177	1820
ERA	2.20	2.81

I guess it's nice for people to notice you, but I like to just do my job on the field."
—*Edgar Martinez, Seattle Mariners*

Edgar Martinez

DESIGNATED HITTER—SEATTLE MARINERS

Edgar Martinez is such a pure hitter that he's won two American League batting titles; so gifted, he's batted .338 over the past three seasons.

It seems incredible now that scouts in his native Puerto Rico were reluctant to even give him a tryout, thinking he was too slow, too weak.

It seems even more incredible that Martinez was reluctant to sign the contract that the Seattle Mariners finally offered, fearing he might not succeed.

The year was 1982. Martinez, then 20, was going to college, playing in a semi-pro league, working the night shift in a pharmaceutical factory.

Rather than move to the U.S., Martinez worried that he should keep taking care of the grandparents who had helped raise him. But his older cousin, Carmelo, a former Major Leaguer, talked him into giving baseball a try.

"He was the one who kept saying, 'Take the chance, you can make it,'" Edgar told the *Seattle Times*. "I did not know. Finally, I decided to try it. But Carmelo . . . he kind of made the decision for me."

It was obviously the right decision, but it didn't look that way at first—Martinez, who spoke little English, batted .173 in his rookie season in Bellingham, Washington.

Still, he worked his way through the Minors, made his debut with the Mariners in 1987 and emerged as one of the game's best hitters in the '90s.

"He's so professional," Seattle manager Lou

"He's so professional. Nothing fazes him. He's as cool as a cucumber at the plate."

99

notice you, but I like to just do my job on the field."

And what he does is impossible to ignore: Martinez, 35, is the only right-handed hitter in the past 50 years to win two American League batting titles. He is also one of only five hitters since 1900 to post back-to-back 50-double seasons.

"Edgar solidifies our lineup like no one else," said Mariners shortstop Alex Rodriguez—an impressive statement, considering the Seattle attack also includes Rodriguez, Jay Buhner and Ken Griffey Jr.

Martinez battled injuries early in his career, undergoing two knee operations and another on his shoulder, and missing most of 1993 with a hamstring problem.

Piniella said. "Nothing fazes him. He's as cool as a cucumber at the plate."

Martinez demonstrated that poise in 1995, when his two-run double in the 11th inning of Game 5 won the Division Series against the New York Yankees. His performance that October gained him national attention. But on a team full of glamorous stars, Martinez is humble, reserved.

"I like to get my satisfaction out of the job I do on the field," he said. "I guess it's nice for people to

> "You can't pitch him high because he'll hit it out. And you can't pitch him inside because there ain't no inside."

But in each of the past three seasons, he has hit 25 or more home runs, and produced at least 100 runs, 100 RBIs and 100 walks. Opponents fret over how to get him out.

"I tell my pitchers that the only thing you can do is keep the ball down and away, and when the guy hits it to right for a single anyway, to shake his hand when he gets to first base," Baltimore Orioles manager Ray Miller said.

"That's all you can do. You can't pitch him high because he'll hit it out. And you can't pitch him inside because there ain't no inside."

Martinez, the Mariners' full-time designated hitter since 1995, does not play a position in the field, focusing only on his hitting. Many DHs struggle with the down time between at-bats, but Martinez excels at the mental side of the game, studying pitchers, making adjustments.

"It's not easy," he said. "It's hard to just go and hit, because when you're not going good it can mentally affect you."

Still, Martinez remembers when his life was truly difficult, when he worked at the pharmaceutical factory in Puerto Rico from 11 p.m. to 7 a.m.

His Mariners' tryout was at 8 a.m. on a Sunday. He rushed home from work, grabbed something to eat and put on his baseball uniform.

Fifteen years later, he is at the top of his profession.

"I always remember how close I came to staying to work at the factory," he said. "I see people working regular jobs and realize you never know what is going to happen."

Edgar Martinez/DH—Seattle Mariners

	1997	CAREER
POS	DH	DH/3B
B	R	R
G	155	1091
AVG	.330	.317
AB	542	3818
H	179	1210
2B	35	291
3B	1	12
HR	28	145
RBI	108	592
R	104	708
SB	2	32
BB	119	674
SO	86	551

Pedro Martinez

PITCHER—BOSTON RED SOX

The winner of the 1997 National League Cy Young Award is sometimes mistaken for a batboy.

Moises Alou once described former Montreal teammate Pedro Martinez as "5-foot-5, 120 pounds, or something like that."

"Small?" Houston's Jeff Bagwell asked. "He looks like Tony Gwynn's 14-year-old son and he's throwing 100 mph."

Martinez, 26, is listed at 5-foot-11 and 170 pounds, but those numbers might be exaggerated. Atlanta pitcher Tom Glavine called him, "just a little beanpole, really."

Most power pitchers are physically imposing—think of Randy Johnson's height, Roger Clemens' thick torso, Nolan Ryan's sturdy legs. Martinez is the exception. He's slight, he throws hard, and he's durable, too.

When the Boston Red Sox signed him to a six-year contract after acquiring him from Montreal, general manager Dan Duquette said he had the potential to be as successful as four-time Cy Young winner Greg Maddux.

Martinez won his first Cy Young at the same age as Maddux, finishing 17-8 last season with a 1.90 ERA and 305 strikeouts. His record might have been better, but the Expos scored only 10 runs in his eight losses.

Perhaps it is fitting that Martinez wound up in Boston, where the passion for baseball is comparable to that in his native Dominican Republic.

[*"He looks like Tony Gwynn's 14-year-old son and he's throwing 100 mph."*]

Ever since I knew I was alive, I played baseball." —*Pedro Martinez, Boston Red Sox*

When it comes to pitching,
few stand taller.

Expos. He would root for Ramon even against his own team, praying for him in the dugout, cheering for him openly on the clubhouse TV.

"You have to know what we lived through to understand why we feel like that," said Pedro. "It's a blood thing. We're too close."

"If I had to give up my career for Ramon to go on, I would do that. To be honest, that's how much he means to me. You have to understand what Ramon

"Ever since I knew I was alive, I played baseball. I played everywhere, in my little room we had, the backyard of the house. I'd accidentally hit people playing in the streets."

Martinez, the fifth of six children, would even remove the heads of his sisters' dolls when he needed balls. He also used rolled-up socks, fruits and rocks—anything he could find.

His father, Paulino, was a successful amateur pitcher in the Dominican Republic. His older brother, Ramon, is the Los Angeles Dodgers' ace. His younger brother, Jesus, is a Minor League pitcher for the Dodgers.

Pedro, too, began his career with the Dodgers, and he cried the day the team traded him to the Expos in 1993. He so idolized Ramon as a young boy that he'd walk miles to see his games, even carry his equipment bag.

Nothing changed after he was traded to the

has done, not only for me, but for my family. He's been like my father sometimes."

The Martinez brothers actually faced each other on August 29, 1996. Pedro struck out 12 and pitched a complete game. But Ramon earned the 2-1 victory.

Today, Pedro is the bigger star, the successor to Clemens as the Red Sox ace, the pitcher expected to lead Boston to its first world championship since 1918.

"He's got what I call a good cockiness about him, a supreme confidence," Dodgers pitching coach Dave Wallace said.

"I remember seeing him pitch in a playoff game his first year in Great Falls, Montana . . . and he was going against a lot of older players. This kid just dominated them. You could see in the lower Minor Leagues there was something special about this guy."

Earlier in his career, Martinez drew criticism for throwing inside and occasionally hitting batters. But his maturity and intelligence are now considered two of his biggest strengths, even if he still looks like a teenager.

"It's a crying shame when the best pitcher in the league has two hairs on his chest," said former reliever Lee Smith, whose professional career began when Martinez was three years old.

Pedro Martinez is still young. He'll probably always be slight. But when it comes to pitching, few stand taller.

Pedro Martinez/RHP—Boston Red Sox

	1997	CAREER
W	17	65
L	8	39
PCT	.680	.625
G	31	185
SV	0	3
IP	241.1	912.1
H	158	702
R	65	338
ER	51	304
BB	67	306
SO	305	970
ERA	1.90	3.00

The first five years I played strictly on physical ability. Then I realized the mental aspect of the game." —*Mark McGwire, St. Louis Cardinals*

Mark McGwire

FIRST BASE—ST. LOUIS CARDINALS

He is this generation's Babe Ruth. Mark McGwire hits the most home runs and the longest home runs in baseball. And like the Babe before him, he has a soft spot for children.

As legend has it, Ruth once promised to hit a home run for a boy in a hospital, then delivered that day. McGwire makes less flamboyant promises. But when he fulfills them, he changes people's lives.

The day he signed with the St. Louis Cardinals, McGwire announced he was creating a foundation to help abused children. He was so overcome by the moment, he started to cry. For half a minute, he could not even speak.

"Oh, wow," the 6-foot-5, 245-pound slugger said after finally composing himself. "Sorry about that. It's just, oh, wow, let's just say children have a special place in my heart."

That became apparent with one game left in the 1987 season, when McGwire had 49 home runs. Rather than go for No. 50, he boarded a plane so he could be present for the birth of his son, Matthew.

"You'll always have a chance to hit 50 home runs. You'll never have a chance to have your first child again."

And yet, for the longest time, it appeared that McGwire might not improve on his spectacular rookie year with the Oakland A's.

He hit 40 homers only once over the next eight seasons. His batting average declined, bottoming out at .201 in 1991. And then there were his injuries, one after another.

He hits the most home runs and the longest home runs in baseball.

McGwire, 34, has hit 387 career homers, but that number would have been considerably higher if he had stayed healthy. By now, he might have passed 500, and stood a chance of becoming only the fourth player in history to reach 600.

Instead, he missed 20 games with a strained rib cage muscle in '92, and that was only the start. McGwire appeared in just 27 games in '93 due to an injured left heel, and only 47 in '94 due to back and heel problems.

"I was down. But I looked at the game of baseball from a different point of view. I got to sit and watch the game. I watched pitchers. I watched hitters. I began to use my mind like I never had."

Still, other players would say, "Imagine what he could do if healthy." McGwire provided a partial answer in '96, crushing 52 homers after missing the first 18 games. He gave the full answer in '97, despite changing leagues at mid-season.

Playing for Oakland, then St. Louis, McGwire matched the Major League record for home runs by a right-handed batter with 58. His 110 homers in consecutive seasons broke a 64-year-old record for a right-handed batter.

Only one other player in history has put together back-to-back 50-homer seasons—Ruth. McGwire's career average of one homer every 11.9 at-bats is second only to Ruth, who averaged one every 11.8.

"I wasn't chasing anybody," McGwire said after hitting the most home runs in the Majors since Roger Maris' 61 in 1961. But in St. Louis, he quickly became a folk hero.

Fans gathered by the thousands to watch McGwire hit mammoth blasts during batting practice. They produced deafening cheers the night he signed a three-year contract—and McGwire responded with a 517-foot home run.

The Cardinals weren't certain they could keep McGwire when they traded for him. McGwire, who is divorced, wanted to play in a city where he could be closer to his son. Matthew, now 10, lives with his mother in southern California.

McGwire, 34, decided to stay only after Matthew made a month-long visit to St. Louis and gave the city his approval. "That had a big part in what I was going to do," McGwire said. "It meant a lot to me."

He signed his contract, then broke down in tears talking about his new charity. McGwire is one of the

biggest men in baseball. But on that day, he attained even greater stature.

"I was literally speechless," McGwire said. "My insides were turning because I wanted so much to help young children."

He is this generation's Babe Ruth, in more ways than one.

Mark McGwire/1B — St. Louis Cardinals

	1997	CAREER
POS	1B	1B
B	R	R
G	156	1380
AVG	.274	.260
AB	540	4622
H	148	1201
2B	27	198
3B	0	5
HR	58	387
RBI	123	983
R	86	811
SB	3	10
BB	101	890
SO	159	1104

Paul Molitor

DESIGNATED HITTER—MINNESOTA TWINS

Few 20-year veterans play better in the second half of their career than they did in the first. Paul Molitor is an exception.

In his first nine seasons, Molitor batted .291. In his last 11, he has batted .319. "I underestimated the way he'd keep going, because I was struggling at 36 and 37," said Molitor's former teammate, Robin Yount. "You're supposed to be declining after you're 35. That's the most amazing thing about his career to me."

Molitor, 41, is perhaps best known for his 39-game hitting streak with Milwaukee in 1987, the seventh longest in Major League history. He was also the Most Valuable Player of the 1993 World Series with Toronto, and he reached 3,000 hits in '96 with his hometown Minnesota Twins.

Still, his biggest accomplishment might be the way he has sustained a career that once appeared doomed by injuries.

You name it, Molitor hurt it—his rib cage, ankle and wrist; his elbow, hamstring and ring finger; his thumb, knuckle and forearm. He was on the disabled list 10 times in the '80s, and has missed 683 games— more than four seasons' worth—due to injuries and work stoppages.

If he had stayed reasonably healthy, he would have ranked even higher than 12th on the all-time hit list, but Molitor doesn't look back longingly on the time he lost.

"It's never with a sense of regret or bitterness. It's

He's not getting older,
he's getting better.

110

I really try to enjoy, savor and give as much as I can as this winds down." *— Paul Molitor, Minnesota Twins*

Molitor is the only player in Major League history to attain 3,000 hits, 450 steals and 200 home runs.

97 percent of his team's games. And his numbers started to build.

Molitor is the only player in Major League history to attain 3,000 hits, 450 steals and 200 home runs, a reflection of his speed, power and batting skill.

Over the past five seasons, his .351 average with runners in scoring position is the second highest in the Majors, behind only Tony Gwynn's .387.

Not bad, considering he was 37 when that spectacular run of clutch hitting started. When Molitor

more just, hmmm, it would have been fun to see what could have happened. But when you're lucky enough to play 20 years and experience some of the things I've experienced, there's not a lot of room for feeling sorry for yourself."

Over the years, Molitor developed one of the most distinctive batting styles in baseball—he stands perfectly still at home plate, then unleashes a quick, compact swing.

He hits for average. He hits to the gaps. He hits in the clutch. He hits anywhere and everywhere, and his consistency, resiliency and integrity make him one of the most respected players in the game.

Molitor played all four infield positions and the outfield early in his career, but he has been his healthiest—and most productive—as a designated hitter.

The DH role protects him, enabling him to avoid injuries in the field. From 1991 to 1996, he played in began his career in 1978, Seattle's Alex Rodriguez was three years old.

"Every day I come out here, I realize I'm one day closer to not being able to do this again," Molitor said. "That reality is more clear now than it's ever been, so I really try to enjoy, savor and give as much as I can as this winds down."

There is much for Molitor to savor—his World Series appearances with Milwaukee in '82 and Toronto in '93, his 39-game hitting streak that is the game's longest in 20 years and now his return home to Minnesota.

Molitor grew up in St. Paul and attended the University of Minnesota. His brother and six sisters live in the Twin Cities. His father, Dick, is nearing 70. "I wanted him to hop in the car and drive to the ballpark, like the old days," Molitor said.

Little did he know that his family would be seeing him at his best. Since 1991, Molitor has raised his career batting average from .299 to .308. Most players start to fade by the time they approach 3,000 hits. Molitor led the American League with a career-high 225 hits the season he reached 3,000.

He's not getting older, he's getting better. If Paul Molitor is a throwback, why does it seem like he should play forever?

Paul Molitor/DH—Minnesota Twins

	1997	CAREER
POS	DH	DH/1B/OF
B	R	R
G	135	2557
AVG	.305	.308
AB	538	10,333
H	164	3178
2B	32	576
3B	4	109
HR	10	230
RBI	89	1238
R	63	1707
SB	11	495
BB	45	1049
SO	73	1203

Mike Mussina

PITCHER–BALTIMORE ORIOLES

Mike Mussina is defined not by his dazzling knuckle-curveball, his lofty winning percentage or his spectacular 1997 Post Season.

No, the Orioles' right-hander is defined by a town of about 5,000 three hours from Baltimore—Montoursville, Pennsylvania.

Mussina, 29, was born and raised there. He still returns there in the off-season. He plans to retire there, too.

His parents live in Montoursville. His wife is from Montoursville. And Mussina signed his latest contract for significantly less money than he could have received as a free agent because he wanted to stay close to his hometown.

"It's not large by any means," Mussina said. "You can get from one side of town to the other in about five minutes by car—maybe three minutes, if you don't hit any lights."

Montoursville is located 10 miles east of Williamsport, home of the Little League World Series. Mussina was a three-sport star in high school. He declined a kicking scholarship to Penn State to play baseball at Stanford.

He's slightly built at 6-foot-1 and 185 pounds, and he doesn't look much like a ballplayer, really. Still, Mussina is such a good athlete that he's won two Gold Gloves for his fielding, and hit a single off the Atlanta Braves' John Smoltz in his first inter-league game.

Pitching, though, is his true calling, the perfect

> *Mussina is such a good athlete*
> *that he's won two Gold Gloves*
> *for his fielding.*

114

You don't get any extra bonus points for doing all right personally. You win or you lose."
— *Mike Mussina, Baltimore Orioles*

career choice for a small-town kid with a fiercely competitive spirit and an active mind.

Mussina is so intelligent, he earned an economics degree from Stanford in 3½ years. He can out-think hitters by mixing his pitches, or he can overpower them with 90-mph fastballs.

His career .682 winning percentage is the highest among active pitchers. And last May, he came within two outs of pitching a perfect game against Cleveland, the eventual American League champion.

Still, for all Mussina's accomplishments, it took four stunning performances in the 1997 Post Season for him to be truly recognized among the game's elite.

First, he beat Randy Johnson twice in the Division Series, lifting the Orioles over powerful Seattle. Then came the American League Championship Series against Cleveland, and Mussina raised his game again. He allowed only one run in 15 innings, but somehow, the Orioles lost both games and the series.

"I'm not disappointed for him," Orioles center fielder Brady Anderson said. "I feel great for him. He proved he's truly a great pitcher in this Post Season. I'm glad everyone got to see him."

> *His career .682 winning percentage
> is the highest among active pitchers.*

Mussina set a Post Season record by recording 41 strikeouts in his four starts. Three October legends— Bob Gibson, Tom Seaver and Orel Hershiser— shared the previous mark.

Seattle shortstop Alex Rodriguez said Mussina pitched like "a four- or five-time Cy Young winner." Cleveland manager Mike Hargrove said no pitcher had dominated the Indians like the Orioles' ace.

"What more could he have done?" left fielder B.J. Surhoff asked after the Orioles were eliminated. "Shoot, he carried us on his back. He was fantastic."

Mussina, though, saw no reason to celebrate.

"You don't get any extra bonus points for doing all right personally," he said. "You win or you lose. We lost."

Indeed, Mussina isn't about to get carried away by personal success. He's a four-time All-Star, but he has yet to win 20 games or a Cy Young Award, and remains grounded by his Montoursville roots.

Every off-season, Mussina returns home to help coach the high school football and basketball teams at his alma mater, Montoursville, H.S.

And in August, 1996, he left the Orioles briefly to attend a memorial service for the 16 high school students and five adults from Montoursville who were killed in the explosion of TWA Flight 800.

"There's only 5,000 of us who live there, and when you come from a place that small, you're supposed to be there when they need you," Mussina said.

Two days later, he shut down the Mariners at Camden Yards.

Big-time pitcher, small-town heart.

Mike Mussina/RHP — Baltimore Orioles

	1997	CAREER
W	15	105
L	8	49
PCT	.652	.682
G	33	194
SV	0	0
IP	224.2	1362.1
H	197	1263
R	87	558
ER	80	530
BB	54	328
SO	218	978
ERA	3.20	3.50

Mike Piazza

CATCHER—LOS ANGELES DODGERS

As a boy growing up outside of Philadelphia, Mike Piazza would hit 300 baseballs a day in a batting cage his father made out of scrap wood.

Vince Piazza would tell his son, "If you work hard, dreams do come true. Always believe in yourself, even when others don't. Look for an opportunity, then take it."

Simple advice, perhaps, but Mike Piazza is living proof of the American dream—and so is his father.

Vince was a high-school dropout who built a mammoth business empire. Mike was a 62nd-round draft pick who became the best-hitting catcher in the Major Leagues.

"I definitely got my drive from my father. He has shown me what I can accomplish through hard work. I know if I didn't have the determination of my father, I wouldn't be here today."

Indeed, the Los Angeles Dodgers only drafted Piazza in 1988 as a courtesy to former manager Tommy Lasorda. Vince Piazza had asked for a favor. And Vince was an old friend of Lasorda's from Norristown, Pennsylvania.

A total of 1,389 players were picked ahead of Mike, the second of Vince's five sons. Only 43 were selected behind him. The draft no longer even lasts 62 rounds.

"Mike couldn't throw. He couldn't catch the ball. He couldn't run," former Philadelphia pitching coach Johnny Podres once said. "And his bat was so slow, he looked like he was swinging in slow motion."

> *"Always believe in yourself, even when others don't. Look for an opportunity, then take it."*

118

I 'll never take this game for granted. Never." — *Mike Piazza, Los Angeles Dodgers*

Still, Piazza could dream. He grew up idolizing Mike Schmidt. And at the 1996 All-Star Game in Philadelphia, guess who caught the ceremonial first pitch from Schmidt and was named the game's Most Valuable Player? "I begged the Dodgers to draft him. But Mike's the one who's taken advantage," Lasorda said that night from a Los Angeles hospital, where he was recovering from a heart attack.

Not that Piazza had it easy. He spent one winter playing in the Dominican Republic, another in Mexico. And he almost quit early in his career, angered by the jealousy that resulted from his close ties with Lasorda.

If you work hard, dreams do come true. By his third pro season, Piazza was the leading home-run hitter in the Dodgers' Minor League system. By his fourth, he was in the Major Leagues.

Since then, he has produced five straight outstanding seasons—his .337 batting average over that stretch ranks second only to Tony Gwynn's .368. And in 1997, Piazza reached for even greater heights.

His 40 home runs tied the second-highest total by a catcher in Major League history. His .362 batting average was the highest by a catcher in 61 years. His 201 hits

"He's one of the stronger guys in baseball. Nobody else hits most of his home runs to the opposite field."

were the most ever by a player who caught 130 or more games.

"You've had just a few great catchers: Bench, Dickey, Cochrane, Berra, Lombardi," Hall of Famer Ted Williams said. "Piazza hits with the best of them."

The physical demands of catching often wear down a player and affect his hitting. But the 6-foot-3, 215-pound Piazza actually got stronger in 1997, leading the National League in batting average, home runs and RBIs after the All-Star break.

"I've never seen anybody do it the way he does it," Atlanta manager Bobby Cox said at the '96 All-Star Game. "He hits down on the ball, but he gets backspin. That makes the ball carry.

"He's one of the stronger guys in baseball. Nobody else hits most of his home runs to the opposite field. And I mean 450-foot homers."

But Piazza, 29, doesn't rely solely on ability. He adheres to a rigorous off-season regimen, largely forsaking the fast-paced Los Angeles lifestyle to focus on his hitting and conditioning.

"I'll never take this game for granted. Never," Piazza said. "I've worked too hard to get here. It's something I've always been taught, and lived by. I know this can be gone as easily as it comes."

He remembers those long hours hitting in the batting cage. He remembers getting drafted in the 62nd round. *If you work hard, dreams do come true.* Mike Piazza is living proof.

Mike Piazza/C — Los Angeles Dodgers

	1997	CAREER
POS	C	C
B	R	R
G	152	689
AVG	.362	.334
AB	556	2558
H	201	854
2B	32	110
3B	1	3
HR	40	168
RBI	124	533
R	104	423
SB	5	10
BB	69	272
SO	77	413

"**I**f someone asked me when I started if I thought anyone could play 2,000 straight games, I'd have said no."
—*Cal Ripken Jr., Baltimore Orioles*

Cal Ripken, Jr.

Breaking Lou Gehrig's consecutive-games record made him an instant legend, a national hero, a symbol of all that was right in sports.

Yet, Cal Ripken has been so celebrated since the magical night of September 6, 1995, that people forget what made his streak possible in the first place.

It wasn't his physical strength, mental toughness or amazing luck. It was his greatness as a baseball player.

If Ripken hadn't been skilled enough to win two Most Valuable Player Awards, appear in 15 straight All-Star Games and set numerous hitting and fielding records, perhaps one of his managers would have given him a day off.

But at the age of 37, after 2,478 consecutive games, he was one of the Baltimore Orioles' best players in the 1997 Post Season. And even without The Streak, he likely would be headed to the Hall of Fame.

Few fans recall that Lou Gehrig, the original Iron Man, had seven seasons with 150 or more RBIs. And few grasp that Ripken was a revolutionary figure in the sport.

Ripken was the tallest regular shortstop in Major League history, the best power-hitting shortstop and a top-fielding shortstop before moving to third base in 1997.

At 6-foot-4 and 225 pounds, he redefined a position once reserved for slightly-built singles hitters, and set the standard for a generation of slugging shortstops who followed.

This "Iron Man" broke one of baseball's most fabled records.

123

Aberdeen, Maryland, which is about 30 miles north of Baltimore. His father, Cal Sr., spent 37 years as a player, coach and manager with the Orioles' organization.

Like Robinson, Ripken made it his goal to play his entire career in Baltimore. But there's one Major difference between the two Orioles' legends:

Ripken is a better hitter.

He holds the Major League record for home runs by a shortstop (345). In 16 seasons, he has averaged 23 homers and 91 RBIs, and batted .276.

Before Ripken, players like Alex Rodriguez and Derek Jeter might have been outfielders, third basemen, even pitchers. But Ripken proved it was possible for a big man to play short.

He didn't have the range of an Ozzie Smith, but he studied hitters' and pitchers' tendencies, and he always seemed to be in the right place at the right time.

In 1990, his superior positioning ability, combined with his sure hands and powerful arm, helped him set a Major League record for the fewest errors by a shortstop.

Hall of Fame third baseman Brooks Robinson once made as many errors in an inning—three—as Ripken made that year.

Ripken idolized Robinson growing up in

> *On the field?*
> *He's simply indestructible.*

And yet, those numbers don't fully explain Ripken's importance to the Orioles, or to baseball.

Ripken's pursuit of Gehrig—and the emotional record-breaking game at Camden Yards—helped revive fan interest after the players' strike of 1994-95.

He remains one of the game's ambassadors, sign-

ing autographs in every city he visits, displaying many of the virtues often missing in today's athletes.

On the field?

He's simply indestructible.

In 1996, Ripken set a world record by playing in his 2,216th consecutive game. The previous mark was held by third baseman Sachio Kinugasa, who played with the Hiroshima Carp in Japan's Central League.

Even when Ripken's not hitting, he's an asset defensively. And even in those rare times when he struggles with his glove—as he did initially at third base in 1997—his presence alone inspires his team.

"When you have Cal on your team, that rubs off on other players," Orioles center fielder Brady Anderson said.

Such is Ripken's dedication, he rarely even misses infield practice. He slumped while playing through a debilitating back injury at the end of the 1997 season. But just when it appeared time for him to finally sit down, he revived in the playoffs, leading the Orioles with a .385 batting average.

"He has to be as strong mentally as anybody who has ever played this game," said former Detroit Tigers shortstop Alan Trammell, who spent 20 years in the Majors but never played a full season.

That mental strength, more than anything, is Ripken's trademark. He never forgot his first two months with the Orioles in 1981. He was a bench player, not a regular.

[*"He's going to play until he stops breathing."*]

"I really do remember thinking to myself, even back then, that if I ever got a chance to get back into the lineup, I was not coming out," Ripken said.

The Streak began the following season, on May 30, 1982. Ripken broke Gehrig's record on September 6, 1995—13$\frac{1}{2}$ seasons later.

Since then, he has played in 346 straight games. That alone would be the second-longest current streak, behind Houston's Jeff Bagwell (351).

Ripken has always maintained that the streak was merely a product of his desire to play everyday. But if he'd been a .220 hitter or error-prone fielder, one of his managers would have benched him long ago.

"I always knew Cal was a good player, but I never

knew how great a player he is until I got the chance to play with him day after day," said first baseman Rafael Palmeiro, who joined the Orioles prior to the 1994 season.

"He's so steady. If you saw him play once or twice, he might not amaze you, but if you see him day after day, you appreciate all the little things he does to help his team win."

How long can Ripken keep going? Well, he'll be 39 at the end of his current contract, but he stays in such excellent shape that it's possible he'll play into his 40s.

"He's going to play until he stops breathing," Orioles pitcher Mike Mussina said. "We're going to wheel him out there in a wheelchair, he'll move himself into position, be right there when the ball comes, and throw the runner out at first."

Would anyone be surprised?

Cal Ripken, Jr. always plays the game right.

Cal Ripken/3B — Baltimore Orioles

	1997	CAREER
POS	3B	SS/3B
B	R	R
G	162	2543
AVG	.270	.276
AB	615	9832
H	166	2715
2B	30	517
3B	0	43
HR	17	370
RBI	84	1453
R	79	1445
SB	1	36
BB	56	1016
SO	73	1106

y mom is the whole story of my life. She's my whole inspiration." —*Alex Rodriguez, Seattle Mariners*

Alex Rodriguez

SHORTSTOP—SEATTLE MARINERS

Alex Rodriguez is the All-Star you could take home to mother.

He acts polite, humble and respectful. He's deeply religious, possesses movie-star looks and loves his mom.

And don't forget that he hugs children, thanks reporters and praises teammates—even when it costs him Most Valuable Player votes.

"I really feel that I've been given this gift, that I've been blessed," Rodriguez said. "I thank the Lord for that, but I try to remember that it can be taken away, too."

Perhaps, but many in baseball believe that the Seattle Mariners' prodigy is capable of becoming the greatest shortstop ever to play the game.

In a 1996 poll of the 14 American League general managers, six named Rodriguez as the player they would select to start an expansion team.

"The way he's going, someday he might bat .400 and hit 60 home runs," Boston GM Dan Duquette said. "He's the best young talent I've seen in years."

Rodriguez, 22, deflects such talk, saying, "I just want to be the person I am. I don't want to project anything."

His boyhood idols were Cal Ripken and Dale Murphy, two of the game's leading role models. He plays Ripken's former position, wears Murphy's No. 3, and does both of them proud.

Teammates rave about his maturity. Coaches love the way he keeps trying to learn. And Ripken speaks

Rodriguez is capable of becoming the greatest shortstop ever to play the game.

129

handed hitter in 57 years, made him the third youngest AL batting champion, behind Ty Cobb and Al Kaline.

So, why didn't Rodriguez win MVP? Partly because Juan Gonzalez produced his own impressive numbers. And partly because Rodriguez campaigned for his teammate, Ken Griffey Jr.

"How can I be considered MVP of the league when I'm not even the MVP of this room?" Rodriguez would ask, never considering that he would lose the closest MVP vote since 1960.

[*"He has talent that flows with every action."*]

almost with envy about his ability.

"I doubt that I had that much talent coming in," Ripken said. "He has talent that flows with every action."

With that talent, Rodriguez became the first player chosen in the 1993 draft, and produced one of the all-time great offensive performances by a shortstop three years later.

In his first full season, Rodriguez set new standards at his position in runs, hits, doubles, extra-base hits and slugging percentage, and matched Ernie Banks' record for total bases.

His .358 batting average, the highest by a right-

He didn't complain about the result; his mother, Lourdes Navarro, probably would have scolded him. She lives near Rodriguez in Seattle, cooks for him, does his laundry. "I'm lost without her," he said.

Rodriguez, the youngest of three children, was born in New York, lived briefly in the Dominican Republic, then moved to Miami. His father, Victor, a former catcher in the Dominican, left the family when Alex was in fifth grade.

Navarro worked as a secretary and waitress to support her family. She sacrificed enough for Rodriguez to attend a private high school. She served as both his mother and father, and his best friend.

"My mom is the whole story of my life. She's my whole inspiration," Rodriguez said. "If there were hard times, I wasn't aware of them. She deserves everything, she's done so much for me."

And now, she's getting her just reward.

Rodriguez's second season wasn't as spectacular as his first, due in part to a rib cage injury. But he still batted .300 with 23 homers and 84 RBIs, became only the second Mariner to hit for the cycle and led the club with 29 stolen bases.

If anything, his best years should be ahead of him. Shortstops Nomar Garciaparra and Derek Jeter, the last two AL Rookies of the Year, are both older than Rodriguez.

"He wants to be the best player in the game, ever.

He won't tell anyone that, but I know that's how he feels," Mariners second baseman Joey Cora said.

He is the All-Star who seems too good to be true. The All-Star you could take home to mother.

Alex Rodriguez/SS — Seattle Mariners

	1997	CAREER
POS	SS	SS
B	R	R
G	141	352
AVG	.300	.306
AB	587	1384
H	176	424
2B	40	100
3B	3	6
HR	23	64
RBI	84	228
R	100	260
SB	29	51
BB	41	109
SO	99	265

Ivan Rodriguez

CATCHER—TEXAS RANGERS

Johnny Bench was perhaps the greatest all-around catcher in Major League history. And Ivan Rodriguez is the closest thing today to Johnny Bench.

No catcher throws better. Few catchers hit better. And if that's not enough, Rodriguez runs well, plays every day and is still only 26 years old.

"He's not only the best catcher since Johnny Bench, but maybe before Johnny Bench and during Johnny Bench," said Texas manager Johnny Oates.

Like Bench, Rodriguez won six Gold Gloves and appeared in six All-Star Games by the time he was 25. If he plays another decade, who knows what he might accomplish?

"There's no question he's the top catcher of this era," said former Kansas City manager and Gold Glove catcher Bob Boone. "If he can duplicate what he's been doing for a long time, he will be in the Hall of Fame."

Rodriguez, nicknamed "Pudge" by a youth-league coach in Puerto Rico, has increased his batting average in all but one of the last six seasons. But the most fascinating part of his game remains his wondrous right arm.

Opposing baserunners are afraid to even take a lead on Rodriguez, much less steal. Rodriguez will pick them off any base. He'll even throw them out trying to advance on an apparent wild pass or passed ball.

"I call it the Drop Anchor Effect," said Rangers

[
No catcher throws better.
Few catchers hit better.
]

132

I just try to do my best and play hard every day. Every day you play in this league you learn some new things."
— Ivan Rodriguez, Texas Rangers

irst. Drop
second."
guez has led the
tage. Over his
n out nearly half of
ɔ have attempted to

A few years back, Milwaukee manager Phil
Garner kept sending runners on Rodriguez,
figuring the young catcher would crack. Garner no
longer employs such tactics. Rodriguez is too good.

His arm alone would make him a treasured asset,
given the shortage of quality catchers in baseball.
But the 5-foot-9, 210-pound Rodriguez is also a
record-setting offensive player.

His 44 doubles as a catcher in 1996 broke the previous mark of 42 set by Mickey Cochrane in 1930. His
116 runs scored matched Yogi Berra's 1950 mark for
the most by a player serving primarily as a catcher.

Rodriguez wasn't quite as productive last season,
but he established career highs in both batting average (.316) and home runs (20). Oates believes
Rodriguez could hit 30 homers if he sacrificed average for power, and steal 20 bases if asked.

"There's nobody like him," said Oates. "Take all
the tools—catching, throwing, arm strength, hitting
for average, hitting with foot speed—and nobody is
higher, across the board."

Rodriguez is also unusual off the field, especially
for the attention he devotes to children. He gives his

> *"There's nobody like him.
> Take all the tools...and nobody is
> higher, across the board."*

time at youth baseball clinics. And he gives money through the Ivan Rodriguez Charitable Foundation, which benefits underprivileged and cancer-stricken children in the Dallas–Fort Worth area and Puerto Rico.

It sounds strange, but perhaps the only thing that can stop Rodriguez now is his love for the game. He plays more innings than any catcher, and his home games are in the Texas heat. Some fear he might eventually wear down.

That would end the Bench comparisons, but for now they're unavoidable. Bench hit for more power. Rodriguez hits for a higher average. Bench won a record 10 Gold Gloves as a catcher. Rodriguez is now just four short.

"I leave that (talk) to people who know the game. I

just try to do my best and play hard every day.

"Every day you play in this league you learn some new things. There's plenty more for me to learn. It makes me feel good when people say that, but I want to stay [at the top]."

Ivan Rodriguez/C — Texas Rangers

	1997	CAREER
POS	C	C
B	R	R
G	150	880
AVG	.313	.290
AB	597	3264
H	187	948
2B	34	192
3B	4	15
HR	20	88
RBI	77	417
R	98	445
SB	7	26
BB	38	181
SO	89	419

I'm a better person. I'm more at peace with myself." — *Gary Sheffield, Florida Marlins*

Gary Sheffield

OUTFIELD—FLORIDA MARLINS

His off-the-field problems are well-documented. His 1997 regular season was a disappointment. But at the end of the World Series last October, Gary Sheffield whispered to a reporter, "It was worth it . . . all of it."

Worth the difficult climb toward maturity. Worth the frustration of trying to fulfill a landmark contract. Worth the journey, from Milwaukee to San Diego to Florida.

In 1988, Sheffield rode the New York Mets' team bus to a playoff game with his uncle, Dwight Gooden. In '97, he drove the expansion Marlins to a world championship in only their fifth season of existence.

Sheffield, 28, batted only .250 with 21 homers and 71 RBIs during the regular season, mostly because he grew impatient with a lack of good pitches to hit. But he revived in September, just in time to became a Post Season hero.

"It's nice for Gary to start anew, because none of that negative stuff carries over into the Post Season," third baseman Bobby Bonilla said after the Division Series. "He's trying to make everybody forget his regular season."

Over the course of four spectacular weeks, Sheffield did. He stayed patient, drawing 20 walks in 16 games. And he also delivered crucial hits, batting .320 with three home runs and seven RBIs.

His highlights included a game-saving catch in right field in Game 3 of the World Series, and a

> He drove the expansion Marlins to a world championship in only their fifth season of existence.

Last season, the attention finally shifted to baseball, but not in the way Sheffield would have preferred.

He hit half as many home runs as he did in '96, batted 64 points lower and had nearly 50 fewer RBIs. Still, he finished third in the NL with 121 walks and fifth with a .424 on-base percentage. His biggest challenge was learning to accept pitchers working around him, even in a revamped Marlins' lineup.

"It frustrated me and got me down," Sheffield said. "I lost interest and respect for the game because I never pictured baseball would be played that way. When you aren't getting the opportunity to drive in runs you start hearing negative stuff coming your way. All that plays a factor in your mind."

ninth-inning single, stolen base and headfirst slide for the game-winning run in Game 2 of the Division Series.

"All my years of losing, after seeing my uncle win, seeing how that moment felt to him—he could never explain how good it felt—I finally got in that situation after nine years," Sheffield said.

It was a fitting climax for Sheffield, a right-handed hitter with one of the quickest bats in the game. He won a batting title for San Diego in '92. He had a breakout season for Florida in '96. But he had a reputation as a moody, troubled star.

The Tampa native has been stalked, robbed, harassed and arrested, even shot in the shoulder in an apparent carjacking attempt after the '95 season.

And yet, Sheffield controlled his emotions, in a way he hadn't before. He started reading the Bible after the '95 shooting. Conversations with heavy-weight champion Evander Holyfield over the winter and former teammate Terry Pendleton in the spring inspired him to pursue religion further.

"I'm a better person. I'm more at peace with myself," Sheffield said during spring training. "I know who Gary Sheffield is and what he represents. I know what he means to other people. I don't want to disappoint anybody."

Alas, Sheffield batted .227 in April, .222 in May, .244 in June. He said he was almost too calm at times, but he regained the proper balance by

September, hitting .324 with five home runs to help the Marlins clinch the wild card.

His Post Season performance elevated him, liberated him, validated him. Sheffield had difficulty putting the experience into words, other than to say it was the most fun he has had in his career.

He leaped in joy after scoring the winning run in Game 2 of the Division Series, as if he had been waiting for the moment his entire life. It was all worth it right then. And little did Sheffield know, the best was yet to come.

Gary Sheffield/OF — Florida Marlins

	1997	CAREER
POS	OF	OF/3B/SS
B	R	R
G	135	1026
AVG	.250	.291
AB	444	3659
H	111	1048
2B	22	194
3B	1	14
HR	21	180
RBI	71	621
R	86	603
SB	11	123
BB	121	561
SO	79	440

Frank Thomas

FIRST BASE—CHICAGO WHITE SOX

His nickname is "The Big Hurt." But it might be just as appropriate to call Frank Thomas "The Big Wait."

Thomas can bruise a baseball, all right, but not simply because he is built like a defensive lineman.

No, what makes the Chicago White Sox slugger unique is his patience at the plate. His batting eye is so uncanny, he swings only at pitches he can hit.

Combine that discipline with a 6-foot-5, 260-pound physique, and you've got perhaps the best all-around hitter in the game today.

Thomas, 29, frequently draws comparisons to Hall of Famer Ted Williams. But now, he's creating his own legend.

For seven straight seasons, he has batted .300 or better with 20 or more homers and at least 100 RBIs, 100 runs scored and 100 walks.

No other player in Major League history has done that—not Williams or DiMaggio, not Aaron or Mays.

Throw Thomas strikes, and he'll hit for both average and power. Throw him balls, and he'll trot down to first base with a walk.

"One thing that Frank had more than anybody else was his bat discipline," said Bobby Howard, Thomas' coach at Columbus (Ga.) H.S.

"He could get 0-2 on the best pitchers, then foul off some pitches and work the count to 2-2, then 3-2, and then he's walked.

"As big as he is, and for all the tape-measure home

His batting eye is so uncanny, he swings only at pitches he can hit.

I decided if you can't hit it hard, don't swing at it." — *Frank Thomas, Chicago White Sox*

"I really believe he could win the batting title just about every year," his former White Sox manager, Gene Lamont, once said.

Thomas won his first batting crown last season, and his .330 lifetime average is third among active players, behind only Tony Gwynn (.340) and Wade Boggs (.331).

He is the largest player ever to lead his league in hitting, but "The Big Hurt" isn't simply known for his offensive prowess. He has a big smile, and an even bigger heart.

The Frank Thomas Charitable Foundation is

runs he hits, more than anybody I've seen at any level, he has the best bat discipline. It's just a gift."

Actually, Thomas credits Howard with making him such a smart hitter, instilling the mental toughness he needed to succeed in the Major Leagues.

"I was lazy back then, big time. My coach made me run sprints for every bad pitch I swung at, practice or whatever."

"I had to run a lot of sprints. One day I said, 'I'm never going to run another sprint.' I decided if you can't hit it hard, don't swing at it."

It's a philosophy that continues to serve Thomas well, even though his strike zone is one of the biggest in baseball. In theory, that means he should see more good pitches. In reality, opponents are often afraid to throw him strikes.

Thus, patience isn't simply a virtue for Thomas, it's a necessity. And yet, the two-time American League Most Valuable Player still produces monster offensive numbers every season.

Thomas has averaged 39 homers over the last five years, including the strike-shortened '94 and '95 seasons. But as he puts it, "I consider myself a hitter, not a bomber."

responsible for ticket giveaways, book and toy drives, a charity golf tournament and an annual $50,000 donation to the Leukemia Society of America.

The leukemia donation is especially meaningful to Thomas, who was 10 when he lost his 2-year-old sister, Pam, to the disease. "She's always in the back of my mind," he said.

Today, Thomas is married with three children, and entering the prime of his career. His statistics the past two seasons were comparable to his MVP statistics in '93 and '94. And they're all the more impressive, when you consider that he plays his

home games in pitcher-friendly Comiskey Park.

How scary is "The Big Hurt?"

"If you brought Babe Ruth in here during his prime, half the teams would pitch around him and throw to Frank Thomas," former White Sox manager Terry Bevington once said.

"The other half would pitch around Frank and throw to Babe."

Frank Thomas/1B — Chicago White Sox

	1997	CAREER
POS	1B	1B
B	R	R
G	146	1076
AVG	.347	.330
AB	530	3821
H	184	1261
2B	35	246
3B	0	8
HR	35	257
RBI	125	854
R	110	785
SB	1	18
BB	109	879
SO	69	582

Mo Vaughn

FIRST BASE—BOSTON RED SOX

Here's all you need to know about Mo Vaughn: The day he won his Most Valuable Player Award in 1995, he held his news conference not at Fenway Park, but in a neighborhood facility that houses the Mo Vaughn Youth Center.

"Anything individual that happens to me they should be a part of," the first baseman said, referring to the children in his youth development program. "This is where my heart is. These kids should be involved."

The next night, Vaughn was at it again, serving as the celebrity auctioneer at a charity event for terminally ill children. No one should have been surprised. Vaughn is so active in the community that he's become one of the most popular athletes in Boston history.

The 6-foot-1, 240-pound slugger once sent 250 children to see the *Nutcracker* ballet. He promised and delivered a home run to an 11-year-old boy dying of cancer. He regularly visits schools and hospitals throughout New England.

"I don't think it's an obligation players have. It's just something I've gotten involved with," he said. "For me, it puts life in perspective. This community has been good to me."

Vaughn knows he couldn't make the same impact if he were just an ordinary player. But his three straight 30-homer seasons are an achievement matched by only three other Red Sox—Ted Williams, Jimmie Foxx and Jim Rice.

He is an unmistakable sight at home plate, waving his bat, swaying in his crouch, representing sheer power.

I grew up with the understanding that you're supposed to pass something on." —*Mo Vaughn, Boston Red Sox*

"He has always been a leader. He has that kind of personality. People rally around him."

His '96 season (.326, 44 homers, 143 RBIs) was even better than his MVP performance in the strike-shortened '95 campaign. And his '97 numbers (.315, 35, 96) would have been near that level if he had not missed 21 games with a knee injury.

The mammoth Vaughn is an unmistakable sight at home plate, waving his bat, swaying in his crouch, representing sheer power. He first developed his stance at the age of three, with his mother, Shirley, serving as hitting instructor.

Vaughn grew up in Norwalk, Connecticut, the youngest of three children, and the only son. His father, Leroy, was a high-school principal and football coach. His mother was an elementary-school teacher.

"My father was out coaching his teams, so my mother was the one that taught me the beginning things about all the sports," Mo said. "Left-handed was the only way she knew how to stand, so that's how I stood."

He was an active child—so active, Shirley recalled, that "we had to run him around the block before kindergarten so he could settle down." He had a ball on a rope in his backyard, and he would practice his hitting day and night.

Leroy and Shirley, however, were strict parents, and eventually they sent Mo to Trinity Pawling Prep in Pawling, New York. From there, he attended Seton Hall, where he was an All-American in each of his three seasons.

The Red Sox selected Vaughn with the 23rd pick of the 1989 draft, and he was in the Majors two years later. His career batting average is .298. He had a 40-homer, 200-hit season in '96. Still, he has not forgotten his parents' lessons.

"I know the value of an education," Vaughn said. "My father was a principal. I admit I wasn't the greatest student in the world. I just studied well enough to play sports. But I grew up knowing the difference between right and wrong. I grew up with the understanding that you're supposed to pass something on."

Leroy and Shirley taught him to be honest, and Mo became thoughtful and outspoken. Shirley, in particular, taught him that "regardless of what happens, you are no better than anybody else." Mo practically adopted that as his motto.

He wears No. 42 in tribute to the late Jackie Robinson. He holds baseball clinics all over New England. He has become an immense favorite in Boston.

"He has always been a leader," said John Valentin, a teammate of Vaughn's with the Red Sox and at Seton Hall. "He has that kind of personality. People rally around him."

That's Mo Vaughn. Most Valuable Person. Most Valuable Player.

Mo Vaughn/1B — Boston Red Sox

	1997	CAREER
POS	1B	1B
B	L	L
G	141	892
AVG	.315	.298
AB	527	3219
H	166	960
2B	24	168
3B	0	8
HR	35	190
RBI	96	637
R	91	521
SB	2	28
BB	86	458
SO	154	810

I look back and maybe pat myself on the back a little bit and say, 'Way to go.'"—*Larry Walker, Colorado Rockies*

Larry Walker

OUTFIELD—COLORADO ROCKIES

Larry Walker wanted to be a hockey player. Growing up in western Canada, what young boy didn't?

Walker was a skater, not a slugger. He used a stick, not a bat. His hero was Mike Bossy, not Mike Schmidt.

But when a junior hockey coach kept his nephew over Walker as a backup goalie, hockey's loss became baseball's gain.

Walker was fortunate that the Montreal Expos were so intent on developing a Canadian star that they would sign virtually any young player with raw talent.

But not even the keenest scout could have predicted that 12 years later, he would become the first Canadian to win a Most Valuable Player Award.

"I've done something good for me personally and even better, I've done something good for my country," said Walker, now with the Colorado Rockies.

Walker, 31, is yet another example of the growing international trend in baseball. But unlike players from Latin countries, he didn't grow up living and breathing the sport.

He played fast-pitch softball before he played baseball. And even after the Expos made him a professional, he still wasn't certain of how the game was played.

In his first Minor League season, Walker was running on the pitch and rounding second base when a teammate lined out, forcing him to head back to first.

"He's one of the best baserunners I've ever seen."

Walker did, but not by the conventional route.

He raced back across the infield and over the pitcher's mound, then argued with the umpire who called him out after he "beat" the throw.

Want to know how far Walker has come? Kevin Malone, his former general manager with the Expos, calls him, "one of the best baserunners I've ever seen."

Walker has also earned three Gold Gloves for his play in right field, but it was his hitting that won him the MVP Award, not his baserunning or fielding.

After battling injuries for much of his first eight seasons, Walker played in a career-high 153 games in 1997. The results were downright astounding.

Walker batted .366 with a league-leading 49 homers and 130 RBIs. Only Tony Gwynn had a higher average in the National League. Only Andres Galarraga and Jeff Bagwell had more RBIs.

In fact, only one player in Major League history has ever hit for a higher batting average with as many homers—Babe Ruth. And the Babe only did it twice.

Walker's 409 total bases were the most since Stan Musial's 429 in 1948. His 143 runs were the 10th highest total in NL history. His .720 slugging percentage was the fifth highest.

"Day after day I was shocking myself at the things I did," Walker said. "Each day I went to the park thinking just let my abilities do what they can do. The numbers went up and the balls went out of the park.

"I'd go home at night, back to the hotel room and say, 'Well, I did that again?' I can't believe that. This is fun.'"

Walker even stole 33 bases, becoming only the fifth Major Leaguer with 40 homers and 30 steals in the same season. And unlike previous Rockies' MVP candidates, he could not be considered a creation of hitter-friendly Coors Field—he hit more homers on the road than at home.

> [*Walker hit more homers*
> *on the road than at home.*]

Said Walker's manager, 1979 AL MVP Don Baylor, "He'll find out 18 years from now that you still have that sense of pride, [knowing] that you had that one magical year that solidified you as a great player."

But even after such a season, Walker's fun-loving, free-spirited outlook isn't likely to change. He'll keep bantering with the fans in the right-field seats, remain the same unpretentious kid from Maple Ridge, British Columbia.

Some days, the 6-foot-3, 235-pound Walker still refers to himself as "a little Canadian boy." He never expected to become one of the biggest stars in America's national pastime.

"I look back and see how far I've come in the game, being Canadian and being so far behind most other ballplayers without the high school baseball and college baseball.

"I look back and maybe pat myself on the back a little bit and say, 'Way to go.'"

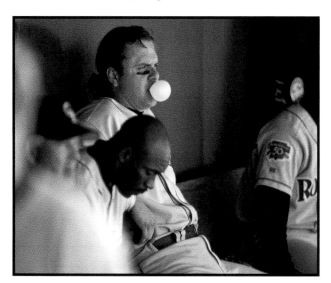

Larry Walker/OF — Colorado Rockies

	1997	CAREER
POS	OF	OF
B	L	L
G	153	1041
AVG	.366	.297
AB	568	3700
H	208	1100
2B	46	242
3B	4	29
HR	49	202
RBI	130	673
R	143	665
SB	33	165
BB	78	411
SO	90	694

I 've always been a player that keeps to himself a lot. I don't make a lot of noise."
— *Bernie Williams, New York Yankees*

Bernie Williams

OUTFIELD—NEW YORK YANKEES

When Bernie Williams gets upset, he doesn't take out his frustrations by yelling at an umpire, throwing his helmet or kicking a water cooler.

He just picks up his guitar.

The New York Yankees' center fielder is a different kind of star, a classically trained musician who hits all the right notes both on and off the field.

Williams, 29, was a top student growing up in Puerto Rico, and still looks bookish in his gold-rimmed glasses. He is so humble and reserved that you would never guess the Yankees consider him the heir to Joe DiMaggio and Mickey Mantle.

Still, there are times when even Williams loses his cool—such as during the 1997 season, when he was sidelined by a chronic hamstring injury.

"My guitar literally saved me from breaking things all around the clubhouse. It saved me from going crazy."

One night after a rainout, Williams organized a jam session in the bowels of Yankee Stadium. Outfielder Paul O'Neill played drums. Kota Ishijima, the former interpreter for pitcher Hideki Irabu, joined Williams on guitar.

"Playing relaxed Bernie," O'Neill said. "The dude is not high strung. If he was any more relaxed, he'd be in a coma."

In a sense, Williams was born to be a Yankee—his parents, Bernabe and Ruffina, met in the South Bronx, and Bernie lived most of his early years on 160th Street, near Yankee Stadium.

He's a classically trained musician who hits all the right notes both on and off the field.

153

Williams' quiet dignity is what sets him apart.

at a conservatory. Williams replied no, he had signed a contract with the Yankees.

"I didn't even know he played baseball," said Flores. "He never said anything. He was very serious, a very quiet boy. He worked very hard, at school and the guitar. There's not many people like him."

The Yankees knew that. They discovered Williams three months before his 17th birthday, the age at which he could legally be signed. They then paid his way to a summer baseball camp in Meriden, Connecticut, so no other team would learn their secret.

Williams became a switch-hitter in his first professional season, and served a five-year apprenticeship in the Minor Leagues before joining the Yankees for parts of the 1991 and '92 campaigns.

From there, he began a gradual climb toward stardom, playing a graceful center field and emerging as one of the sport's most dynamic packages of speed and power.

Williams' game is so well-rounded that he has batted over .300 the past two seasons, with at least 20 home runs, 100 runs scored, 100 RBIs and 15 stolen bases. And he reached those numbers in 1997 despite missing 33 games.

His breakthrough performance, however, came in the '96 Post Season. Williams batted .467 in the Division Series and .474 in the American League Championship Series. And when the Yankees fell behind two games to none in the World Series, he drove in three runs and scored another in Game 3 to ignite their comeback.

It was then that he drew comparisons to the late

After that, the family returned to Puerto Rico. Bernie entered a music school in seventh grade, the year he took up guitar. As a senior, he was named the class' most accomplished musician.

One of Williams' teachers, Eduardo Flores, asked him if he planned to continue his musical education

Roberto Clemente, the greatest player in Puerto Rican history. Roberto Alomar, Ivan Rodriguez and Juan Gonzalez also hail from the island, but Williams' quiet dignity is what sets him apart.

He is married with three children. He plays with a rare determination, yet a special elegance. And when he needs a break from the game, he turns to his guitar.

"I play at home. I have an acoustic guitar and a Stratocaster. I have a little drum machine, a bass player, a four-track recorder. I have a lot of fun."

Whether he's strumming or swinging. Bernie Williams is a virtuoso.

Bernie Williams/OF — New York Yankees

	1997	CAREER
POS	OF	OF
B	S	S
G	129	810
AVG	.328	.292
AB	509	3179
H	167	927
2B	35	183
3B	6	33
HR	21	100
RBI	100	469
R	107	537
SB	15	82
BB	73	421
SO	80	503

Author's Note

Ken Rosenthal, 35, is an award-winning columnist
and radio personality in Baltimore. He was a baseball writer at the *Baltimore Sun*
from 1987 to 1990, and became a general sports columnist in February, 1991. His columns appear
across the country on the *Times-Mirror* wire service. He also has written for
the *Sporting News* and *Baseball America*, and contributed to *MSNBC*.

Rosenthal, a 1984 graduate of the University of Pennsylvania, has been voted
Maryland Sports Writer of the Year by his peers five times in the last seven years.
He was named the city's best sports writer by the *Baltimore City Paper* in 1994,
and by the readers of *Baltimore Magazine* in 1996 and 1997.

He lives in Reisterstown, Maryland, with his wife, Lisa, and their three children,
Sam, 6, Hannah, 5 and Sarah, 2.

Acknowledgements

Virtually all of the quotes in this book first appeared in newspapers and magazines throughout the United States and Canada. The author would like to thank:

Atlanta Journal-Constitution

Baltimore Sun

Baseball Weekly

Boston Globe

Chicago Sun-Times

Chicago Tribune

Cincinnati Enquirer

Cleveland Plain-Dealer

Daily Oklahoman

Dallas Morning News

Denver Post

Ft. Lauderdale Sun-Sentinel

Ft. Worth Star-Telegram

Hamilton Spectator

Houston Chronicle

Los Angeles Times

Miami Herald

Milwaukee Journal

Minneapolis Star-Tribune

Newsday

New York Post

New York Daily News

New York Times

North County Times

Orlando Sentinel

Palm Beach Post

Rocky Mountain News

Sacramento Bee

San Diego Union-Tribune

San Francisco Chronicle

Seattle Post-Intelligencer

Seattle Times

Sports Illustrated

St. Louis Post-Dispatch

The Sporting News

USA Today

Washington Post

Photography